STUDY GUIDES

General Editors: John Peck and Martin ~~Coyle~~

Palgrave Study Guides

A Handbook of Writing for Engineers *Joan van Emden*
Authoring a PhD *Patrick Dunleavy*
Effective Communication for Arts and Humanities Students
   Joan van Emden and Lucinda Becker
Effective Communication for Science and Technology *Joan van Emden*
How to Manage your Arts, Humanities and Social Science Degree
   Lucinda Becker
How to Manage your Science and Technology Degree
   Lucinda Becker and David Price
How to Write Better Essays *Bryan Greetham*
Key Concepts in Politics *Andrew Heywood*
Making Sense of Statistics *Michael Wood*
The Mature Student's Guide to Writing *Jean Rose*
The Postgraduate Research Handbook *Gina Wisker*
Professional Writing *Sky Marsen*
Research Using IT *Hilary Coombes*
Skills for Success *Stella Cottrell*
The Student's Guide to Writing *John Peck and Martin Coyle*
The Study Skills Handbook (second edition) *Stella Cottrell*
Studying Economics *Brian Atkinson and Susan Johns*
Studying History (second edition) *Jeremy Black and Donald M. MacRaild*
Studying Mathematics and its Applications *Peter Kahn*
Studying Modern Drama (second edition) *Kenneth Pickering*
Studying Psychology *Andrew Stevenson*
Teaching Study Skills and Supporting Learning *Stella Cottrell*

Palgrave Study Guides: Literature

General Editors: John Peck and Martin Coyle

How to Begin Studying English Literature (third edition)
   Nicholas Marsh
How to Study a Jane Austen Novel (second edition) *Vivien Jones*
How to Study Chaucer (second edition) *Rob Pope*
How to Study a Charles Dickens Novel *Keith Selby*
How to Study Foreign Languages *Marilyn Lewis*
How to Study an E. M. Forster Novel *Nigel Messenger*
How to Study James Joyce *John Blades*
How to Study Linguistics *Geoffrey Finch*
How to Study Modern Poetry *Tony Curtis*
How to Study a Novel (second edition) *John Peck*
How to Study a Poet (second edition) *John Peck*
How to Study a Renaissance Play *Chris Coles*
How to Study Romantic Poetry (second edition) *Paul O'Flinn*
How to Study a Shakespeare Play (second edition) *John Peck and
   Martin Coyle*
How to Study Television *Keith Selby and Ron Cowdery*
Linguistic Terms and Concepts *Geoffrey Finch*
Literary Terms and Criticism (third edition) *John Peck and
   Martin Coyle*
Practical Criticism *John Peck and Martin Coyle*

HOW TO STUDY
FOREIGN LANGUAGES

Marilyn Lewis

palgrave

Published by
PALGRAVE
Houndmills, Basingstoke, Hampshire RG21 6XS and
175 Fifth Avenue, New York, N. Y. 10010
Companies and representatives throughout the world

PALGRAVE is the new global academic imprint of
St. Martin's Press LLC Scholarly and Reference Division and
Palgrave Publishers Ltd (formerly Macmillan Press Ltd).

ISBN 0–333–73667–2 paperback

This book is printed on paper suitable for recycling and made from fully managed and sustained forest sources.

A catalogue record for this book is available from the British Library.

10   9   8   7   6   5   4
08   07   06   05   04   03

Printed in China

To Rhys and Monica who have helped in so many ways

Contents

PART II STRATEGIES FOR LANGUAGE ACQUISITION

ACKNOWLEDGEMENTS

My thanks are due to all the students who took part in this study. In particular I would like to thank the following who gave extra time: Monica Bayldon for her account of learning Spanish overseas; Adrienne Dench for her reflection on learning Dutch; Jae Ho for his account of what he wants in a grammar book; Gareth Lewis for answering many extra questions; Gong Lidu for his cultural information; Graeme Smith for his mind map and for ideas about learning journals.

In addition I want to offer sincere thanks to three people whose help was vital to completing the project: Breon Gravatt whose ideas and practical help are reflected in both the content and the organisation of the book; Alison Kirkness for her detailed and incisive comments after reading the draft; Rhys Lewis who took time to make computer arrangements when Auckland was hit by an electricity crisis in the final days of this book's preparation.

GENERAL EDITORS' PREFACE

If you are studying a foreign language the chances are that you are looking for a book that will not only help you get to grips with the basic principles of what is involved, but also a book that will help you develop into a successful language learner. The aim of *How to Study Foreign Languages* is to offer you guidance on how to gain both of these important skills by providing the sort of vital practical information you need about how to organise and improve your learning methods and techniques.

The book is divided into two parts. The first part examines what is involved in learning a language, looking both at the broader questions of course design and choice and at successful strategies for learning, including organisation, techniques for remembering, using a journal as well as modern electronic language technology.

The second part focuses on the key practical issues that face all language learners: vocabulary learning, listening to a new language, speaking fluently and learning grammar. In addition, there are chapters on studying literature in a new language, the importance of cultural contexts, and also advice on writing as well as on exams. As with all the chapters of the book, these can be read separately or dipped into for information or guidance.

In the first instance it may well repay you to read quickly through the book as whole, so that you gain a sense of what studying a new language involves. You might then focus on those aspects which interest you most, or use the questionnaire at the end to assess your learning needs. At once a reference guide to ideas about language study and a practical textbook that will develop your skills as a student of language, *How to Study Foreign Languages* is designed to help you get the most out of your course and to achieve excellent results.

JOHN PECK
MARTIN COYLE

AUTHOR'S PREFACE

People used to claim that only really gifted people could learn another language. Apart from the difficulty of defining what is meant by 'gifted' and how success is measured in the end, this is too simple a statement. By observing many adults who change countries, either by choice or by force of circumstances, we can see that with a combination of motivation and work (and even sometimes with a minimum of these!) plus useful learning strategies people of all ages and educational backgrounds do learn second and third languages.

Furthermore, it is not the case that language learners are either successful or unsuccessful, nor that they do or do not have strategies for better learning. Many studies show that everyone can improve the way they learn, with greater emphasis on learners taking responsibility for their own progress, as well as their teachers' need to be aware of what leads to good language learning. Unless this happens, learners will fall into the trap of sticking to familiar routines (such as memorising word lists by covering up one half, for instance) and not knowing how to solve an unfamiliar task when faced with it.

Language learners and their teachers need to know what strategies they have never thought of using. Traditionally success has meant doing well in particular courses of study, and yet from the viewpoint of learners, being able to use the language in out-of-class situations could be a better yardstick. Some learners have reported doing very well in their formal courses but found gaps once they wanted to use the language with native speakers.

This book is written for students who have chosen to study a language in senior secondary schools or as part of a university degree. There are many reasons for choosing a particular language. Some are utilitarian. People believe that knowing a language will find them a better job, or they want to use it for travel, or the regulations say they must study a language as part of their degree. Others have more personal reasons. Perhaps the language they are studying has been spoken by their ancestors or even by their living grandparents. A third group of students just like learning languages. It could be Japanese or Spanish or Latin. It doesn't matter as long as it's a language.

The ideas in this book come from several sources. A number of current and recently graduated students who were classified as 'successful' because of their course grades in languages were willing to answer a fairly lengthy questionnaire. In selecting 'successful' language learners, a decision had to be made as to how these would be defined. We decided that students with high grades in their end-of-year results would be chosen, although it is acknowledged, even by some of the learners, that their formal success did not necessarily make them highly competent outside class.

We wanted answers from a range of languages, so that the examples could be relevant to as many readers as possible. Questionnaires were designed, drawing on an extensive literature on language learning. These were sent to lecturers in five language departments (French, Spanish, Russian, Japanese and Chinese) for distribution amongst their students. Personal contacts were also used. These students' comments about why and how they studied appear throughout this book. Some of the respondents completed information for more than one language, which highlighted an interesting feature. Students didn't always use the same strategies for all the languages they were learning. The students' replies were included even when they clashed with the 'official' advice about language learning. For example, despite the widely held belief by educators that rote learning is unhelpful, many of the language learners in this study reported using it successfully. At least one was aware of the official viewpoint: 'That's supposed to be wrong isn't it?' he said.

Another source of information for the book is all the books and articles for teachers written on the topic of successful language learning, many based on studies with large numbers of students in many parts of the world. Some of these are included in the Further Reading section at the end. They are based on research from many countries into what makes the difference between success and failure in language learning.

The interest in 'learning to learn' has indeed led to a number of publications, most directed at teachers and a few at language learners. Many of these are in the form of tasks for students to do as they consider the language learning process. They have moved beyond the 'Teach yourself' approach where the writer tended to prescribe the learning process. Learners are now invited to assess their progress, evaluate various techniques and draw on many approaches to language learning. Some of the sources listed at the back of this book provide self-checking materials designed to show students what kind of learners they are. They offer general questions designed to identify learning styles and personality traits, and checklists of strategies for students about their own study habits. These strategies may be organisational, social or related to thinking and they cover the areas of grammar, vocabulary, speaking, listening, reading and writing. They are designed to help readers reflect on what they are doing at the moment and to alert them to gaps in their learning strategies.

Why produce another book on the subject if it has already been well addressed by others? This book is not a classroom text in the sense of providing students with things to do. It is a reference book designed either for reading through or, more likely given people's busy schedules, for dipping into as the need arises. The table of contents and the index are meant to help you dip.

The general message of the book is this. You do not have to be brilliantly gifted to be successful at learning a language. You need a combination of motivation and good strategies. Once you have studied a language, so many opportunities are open to you. In the short term, if you have been alerted to the idea of keeping a diary of your own learning strategies, why not make it available to other language learners? The more we know about the range of strategies available, the easier it becomes to pass on to learners information from which they can select and trial ideas that could turn out to be worthwhile. There are many opportunities now through desk-top publishing for spreading good ideas around. At the same time the book is designed to encourage you to enjoy learning your new language. I've tried to keep it as informal as possible while providing the essential information and ideas. I hope you enjoy it.

MARILYN LEWIS

PART I

WHAT IS INVOLVED IN LEARNING A LANGUAGE?

1

Choosing a Language and a Course

> *The first part of this chapter encourages you to think about why you are planning to learn a language. Assuming that you do want to learn a language and you have reached the level of senior secondary school or university in your other studies, how do you choose between all the languages on offer? This chapter has ideas for choosing a particular language and course.*

This chapter looks at answers to questions of why, which and where. Before going into all the suggestions for learning, it is worth taking time to consider why you have chosen to study a language. As we'll see in later chapters, your reasons can affect the way you choose to study. Then you'll be ready to narrow down your choices of language and institution.

1.1 Why learn another language?

Your reason for learning another language will help narrow down your choice of language(s). Here are some of the reasons given by students who took part in our study.

I want it for my future work.
We go there for visits sometimes.
It's a culture that has always interested me.
There are books written in . . . that I want to read in the original.
I really enjoy listening to foreign languages.

3

It should be an easy subject to pick up marks in.
Everyone says it's easy to learn.
My grandmother was Chinese, and that's why I want to learn it.
It's an important language in the world.

Let's consider some of the reasons in detail, using examples that students give, and putting them under broad headings.

Languages for professional purposes

Student 1:   I want to work in India after I qualify. I'll need to learn a language as part of my job.

Students who already know that they want to work in a particular part of the world have an easier choice. Remember, though, that the people there may be bilingual. It's worth finding out what second language they speak. In countries that have had strong trade or colonial ties with other parts of the world it is common to find that some of the population still learn a foreign language to a high level of proficiency. Thus in parts of Africa it is possible to work through the medium of French, German or Portuguese. Tanzania, for instance, has two official languages, Swahili and English. People working in Vietnam in the 1990s have found that even in the same place of work it is common to have someone who speaks French, another who speaks Russian and a third, German, depending on where they have studied abroad or on when they were educated in their own country. Singapore, where many international business people are based, has four official languages: Chinese, Malay, Tamil and English.

Another point to remember is that you could be working with people who do not speak the official language of the country at all, but one of the regional languages. These may differ from one another in their spoken form but not in writing (as in China) or they may be completely different from the official one (as in India). Even without travelling you may find another language useful in your work. In your home country you may plan to work amongst recent immigrants in the areas of health, education or social services. In that case you will want to learn the language spoken by particular groups who use the services you are involved with.

One way to prepare to learn a language for professional purposes is to take a general language course first and then a more specific one which concentrates on the language for particular jobs: tourism, health services, computing and so on.

Languages for everyday living

Student 2:   My parents are going to live in Malaysia for several years. I'd like to learn the language for the times when I'm there on holiday.

This student, and others like her, has a strong reason for learning the language. Making a start on it before you leave home can create goodwill when you first make contacts. The same advice applies here as for the people learning a work language. Make sure that the course you sign on for offers the version spoken currently in your part of the country. Everyday needs will determine your choice, not whether it is widely spoken.

You might prefer a course that concentrates only on the spoken version of the language, so that you can make friends immediately, leaving the written form until later. That is particularly the case if the script is different from your own.

Cultural reasons

Student 3:   As soon as I graduate I plan to go and live in Japan. It's a country I've always admired.

One of the reasons given for learning another language is so that the learner can be part of another culture. Some people want to do more than just live in another country; they want to be a complete part of that culture, perhaps even throwing away aspects of their own culture which they have come to dislike. For example, the person may be converting to another faith or marrying someone of a different culture.

When you ask people years later about the changes they have made, some are delighted with what they have done, while others are pleased to have tried but disappointed with the results. Unless you learn the language very young and spend lengthy periods of time in countries where it is spoken, you will probably continue to feel like a member of your own culture. The complete transformation people hope for doesn't always happen. Regardless of the end result, as a beginning learner you will probably feel slightly disoriented when you choose a course that emphasises cultural learning as well as language growth.

As we shall see in a later section on cross-cultural communication, it is often difficult to sound exactly as you want to sound when speaking a new language. A saying from Ancient China seems relevant here. Two separate entities can combine in such a way that each maintains its original unique characteristics, whereas if either of them is made the same as the other, both degenerate. As a beginning language learner don't be afraid to keep your own characteristics, many of which can contribute to the lives of people you meet when you become part of another speech community.

Languages for reading

Student 4:   Speaking another language doesn't interest me but I'd like to be able to read Russian literature.

This student is one of many people whose purposes are served by learning to read but not to speak. This person may not even be planning to travel. Reading about subjects which have not been translated, or even reading subjects in the original when they have been translated, is a common reason for language learning. Many students of the Classics select Latin, Greek or Hebrew because they enjoy that period of history. Then there are religious reasons for studying ancient languages: Arabic for reading the Koran, Hebrew for the Old Testament and Greek for the New Testament of the Bible.

Languages for enjoyment or a challenge

Student 5:   I just love learning languages. I studied French and German at school and now I'd like to move onto something more challenging.

Student 5 is one of those people who enjoy the sound of a language, reading a new script or even the whole process of learning and trying out another language. They sign on for language courses year after year just for the pleasure and challenge of learning. They may even seek out difficult languages.

Perhaps they are fascinated by some aspect of a language such as the fact that the script is written from right to left as in Arabic or from top to bottom as in traditional Japanese. The whole appearance of a different script can be fascinating. Some language learners take pride in their ability to produce beautiful graphics with a range of pens. These people do not expect to make the same strides within a year as if they were learning a language from the same family group as their own. They want something that will be difficult to master and they are prepared to put the time into it.

Look at examples of several languages with non-Roman scripts before making your choice. In Europe you could consider Russian and Greek or further afield there is Arabic, and the many scripts of India: Hindi (the national language), Urdu, Bengali and so on.

An easy language

Student 6:   I want to learn an easy language. I like the idea of learning a language, but which one would be easiest?

Easy and difficult are subjective terms, but here are some factors that make a language easy or difficult:

The script,
The pronunciation,
Whether it is mainly phonetic,
The textbook,
The amount you are expected to cover in a year.

One way to measure relative difficulty is to find out the level you can expect to reach by the end of the course. You can do this by looking at the final examinations for the previous year in several languages. Compare the difficulty of the passages to be translated from English.

A language very different from your own will be more difficult in some respects but in other ways it will be easy. There is the novelty value and the fact that you will probably put considerable effort into aspects that are new, such as pronunciation or seeing the relationship between characters and their meaning.

Whatever your first language, an obvious place to start the hunt for an easy language is amongst other languages which descend from the same family tree as yours. For English speakers this could mean learning a Scandinavian language or Dutch or German. Such a large proportion of English vocabulary, however, has come either directly or indirectly

from Latin and Greek that languages from these groups could also seem
relatively easy for English speakers. French, Portuguese, Spanish, Italian
and Romanian all have their origins in Latin.

On the other hand, people learning a language very close to their
own, or even very close to another they have learned, say it is easier to
muddle the two. One English-speaking student said she had had to
postpone starting to learn Italian in the same year she started learning
Spanish, for this reason. She found that so many words came from the
common ancestor, Latin, that she kept forgetting which was which. She
also started to confuse the word stress in the two languages.

Family reasons

Student 7:   I want to learn the language my grandparents speak.
There's a lot I want to know about our family history and learning their
language seems like a good start.

When people have strong emotional reasons for learning a language
they find they can overcome many difficulties. In Britain people go to
classes in Welsh or in either Scots or Irish Gaelic for heritage reasons,
while more recent immigrants who do not speak the language of their
parents or grandparents choose to learn Hindi, Arabic and a wide range
of other languages. In other parts of the world, heritage languages
which were once entirely oral are now taught in schools – for instance in
Australia, where there are about 250 Aboriginal languages, some of
which can now be learned in bilingual schools.

Other family reasons include the fact that the learner or one of their
relatives is marrying into another language group, or a child has been
adopted into the family and the family want to support the child in
maintaining links with his or her country of birth. During the 1990s a
number of people have been learning Russian and Romanian for the sake
of the children who have joined their families.

A language for international communication

Student 8:   If I'm going to spend two or three years learning a language
it had better be one that I can use all over the world.

When people say they want to learn a world language, they often mean
they want one where all the effort they put in will have the widest
possible spin-offs. For many types of job, including international diplo-

macy and business, it is difficult to narrow the choice down on that basis. English, French, Spanish, Chinese and Russian are all widely spoken in the world. If you go for popularity by numbers, the languages most frequently spoken as a mother tongue are, in descending order, Chinese, English, Spanish, Hindi, Arabic, Bengali, Russian, Portuguese, Japanese and German. (See Crystal's *Cambridge Encyclopedia of Language* for the rest of the list.) However, if second languages are included, French and Malay are in the top ten ahead of Japanese and German. If a language works for the people who speak it and, in your case, the people from outside who want to communicate with them, then that makes the language important.

1.2 CHOOSING A LANGUAGE

What is a language?

It might seem unnecessary to ask someone who is planning to learn a language whether they know what a language is. The question could perhaps be rephrased as 'When is a language not a language?' The answer is 'When it is a dialect.' Because this is not a book about studying linguistics there is no need to go into technical details here. The main point is that sometimes the language you need or want to learn, although it is not the standard language of the country, is an important dialect which will stand you in good stead in your daily life. For example, Bengali and Assamese are not two separate languages but their identities are reflected in separate labels which are important to their speakers for reasons of their geographic and political identities.

Examples of languages

Keeping in mind your reasons for choosing a language, here is some information about just a few languages which could help you make your choice from the 4,000 to 5,000 available in the world.

The following information is not meant to be exhaustive. If you narrow this number down to those which are actually taught at an institution accessible to you, the choice becomes more manageable.

Chinese has many dialects but the version called Mandarin by English-speaking people is most widely used or at least understood. Amongst Chinese speakers this form is called Putonghua, literally 'common language', although in Taiwan, where it is also used, it has another name. Another popular overseas dialect is Cantonese, which has spread through migration to many of the countries where people from South China have settled. In any case, whichever version you learn, the written form is the same. Many different spoken dialects of Chinese are also spoken outside China. You may be encouraged to hear that in the twentieth century there have been extensive reforms of the Chinese written language which have simplified the form of the characters. The phonetic spelling, or pin-yin, has 58 symbols and is intended to lead people gradually into the standard version.

Japanese has a geographically small home base and yet is often studied by foreigners because of its usefulness for trade. There are three versions of the Japanese script, all pronounced the same. This means that if you are really not interested in reading or writing the language you could choose a course which teaches only spoken communication.

With *ancient languages*, too, you have a choice. Latin, Ancient Greek and Hebrew all have different versions. There is Classical Latin, the language of Ancient Rome. For Hebrew you could choose between the language of the Scriptures and the language spoken in the streets of Israel today. If your ancestors come from the Indian subcontinent you could be interested in learning your ancestral language Sanskrit.

For *Arabic* there is the choice between the Classical Arabic which scholars study in order to read the Quran, and versions of Arabic spoken daily all over the world.

Learning *Malay* would allow you to communicate with millions of people in Indonesia and Malaysia, who use it as either their first or second language. The version known as Bahasa Indonesian is spoken in both countries and is now written in the Roman script.

If you are going to work or live in *India* then you have a choice between learning the national language (Hindi) or the language of the state where you plan to be. Bengali is spoken of course in Bengal but is also the official language of Bangladesh, formerly a part of north-east India. Further west Gujerati and Punjabi are spoken, while in the South there are other quite different languages, including Tamil and Telegu. Once you have taken the trouble to learn one of these languages you will find it of use further afield. The languages of India are spoken in many places beyond the subcontinent, sometimes with a slightly different regional flavour. The descendants of immigrants from the nineteenth century still speak versions of Indian languages in parts of South and East Africa, in parts of the West Indies, and in Fiji, where Hindi is spoken by the many people whose families have lived there for generations alongside the indigenous Fijian-speaking population. In Pakistan, the national language of Urdu, although written in the Arabic script, is effectively the same language as Hindi.

Elsewhere in the *Pacific* there are other languages. Depending on where you plan to travel you could sign up for classes in Fijian, Samoan, Tongan, Niuean or Cook Island Maori, to name just five.

The final choice

The moment has come to narrow down your choice and select the language or languages you want to study. In the end your reasons for studying a particular language will be a combination of what you want, what is possible and what effort you are prepared to put in. If it is going to take years to get to the point where you want to be, then you need to be quite determined in order to get there. The pain will include not only your hours and effort but also your (or someone else's) money. Weigh all the factors and then enjoy your study. We turn now to the question of which type of course will suit you best.

1.3 CHOOSING A COURSE

The next choice you have to make is where to enrol for your language course. As well as courses that are part of a wider programme at school or at university, there are likely to be other options available. The cost and the length of the course will help you make up your mind, but in addition there are particular questions to ask about each. Some of the factors that help people make up their minds about one course or another are dealt with now.

Good teaching

For some people the way the language is taught is the deciding factor. If you have already been recommended a particular language class on the basis of the way it is taught, and you have no other driving force, your choice is easy. The only thing to check is whether the same people will be teaching the course this year as last. Conversely if people try to put you off learning a particular language because of the teachers, you need to balance up your motivation to learn it with the methods that you will be following for one year.

Courses at school and university

The most obvious choice could be to sign on for a language course at the university or school where you are already enrolled and, in fact, most of this book assumes that you will be enrolled in a class. One big advantage of studying with others in a formal course is the motivation. This can include motivation from the teacher, part of whose job is to make the course interesting and worthwhile. Then there is the motivation of your fellow students. Assuming that they are serious about succeeding, there is the motivation from being part of a group who are all aiming at the same goal. Motivation comes, too, from mechanical aspects of a course such as having fixed dates for assignments and tests. You feel some obligation to revise when you know that your grades depend on it.

If you are still at school then your choice is limited to whatever is being offered there that year. However, when it comes to university study there are bigger choices to be made, starting with the choice of a university. Find out which places have a good reputation for languages. In particular, make sure that the language you want continues to be taught at higher levels in case you turn out to be especially interested in continuing.

There are also differences in the way languages are taught at different tertiary institutions, as the following account shows. This student had chosen to learn her ancestral language, Dutch, since she had no knowledge of it at all.

> I learnt Dutch from scratch at——University. Stage I was strictly for those with no Dutch at all and I progressed fairly well coming out with an H3 pass, which in their odd system I guess is equivalent to A–. The emphasis was on grammar and learning to put sentences together and doing grammatical exercises and it suited me because I was excellent at grammar, much better than the younger students who hadn't had formal lessons on the subject. There were no lessons in conversational Dutch, just the exercises in grammar and translations. It was safe and you didn't have to take any risks. As long as you could understand what 'Put the following sentences into the perfect tense' meant and had learnt that week's vocab. you were fine.

Notice that by the end of the first year the student was gaining good marks for doing well the things she was already good at but the skill of actually conversing in Dutch was still beyond her. The second-year course was another story.

> The next year was a shock. Those who knew Dutch went straight into Stage 2 and all of a sudden there were people speaking Dutch in class. No longer could you rely on learning that week's vocab. These people were born knowing that and a good deal more. When asked why they said such and such they would reply, 'Because it sounds right.' To one who required grammatical reasons this was disastrous!

In this second-year class the same phenomenon of reinforcing existing strengths was at work, but for other people. Those who were already fluent speakers of Dutch were able to succeed in a course that valued spoken competence.

> The lecturer taught to the level of those who knew Dutch rather than the ex-Stage 1 people and we couldn't keep up. We'd had no training in conversational Dutch and here it was being used all the time in class and my vocab. was inadequate. I subsided into my shell and hardly opened my mouth and the other ex-Stage 1 did the same.

Notice how easy it was, even for a highly communicative person as this student was, to take the easy way out and remain silent, although everything we know about speaking in a new language suggests that the most successful students are those who give it a go (see Chapter 9). She goes on to describe how it is not necessary to separate grammar learning from communication:

> Yet the emphasis was still on grammar and working through the textbook. I could still hang in there with that. It was the metalanguage[1] that I couldn't understand — the instructions, the wordplay between lecturer and students and I felt really out of it. I remember one day when the lecturer asked me a question in Dutch and I couldn't answer it. He then asked it in simpler form, and simpler form again and I knew what he was doing but even when it got to a stage that I could answer I had completely frozen and wouldn't even have recognised English. What was worse, everyone was being kind and supportive when all I wanted was to be left alone. I did pass at the end of that year but with a C equivalent. Fortunately, the exam was a written one based on translations and grammatical exercises with the instructions in English.

This account shows that even when students know that they are not doing well in one aspect of a course, if the assessment process allows them to build on their strength then they can succeed, or at least, as in this case, gain a pass. By the third year of the course this student was faced with yet another change:

> The next year there was an emphasis on literature, which was o.k. because I could analyse literature quite well but I took ages to read the books. Luckily the lectures were in English.

If studying literature is important to you (or if you would rather confine your studies to the language), then you should be able to find out beforehand whether your goals are the same as those of the course organisers. Ask to see the course outline. You could ask also which language the lectures are given in:

> The language classes, as distinct from the literature ones, were the same as the previous year but I coped better because I had worked out strategies for looking alert and intelligent, yet not contributing or, more importantly, not being asked to contribute. But yet again the emphasis was on working straight through the text book. Forget about the communicative approach! Here I fell down through not understanding the metalanguage although the book work was fine. By this time I was the only ex-Stage I left (what a sucker for punishment) and all the big guns in the class would jabber away in Dutch and ask for explanations on why such and such could or couldn't be used in x, y, z setting.

The proficiency of other students is something you cannot find out beforehand, but in this case the student could judge from the previous year's class that she was likely to be left behind. She is an interesting example of being motivated to the point of continuing despite failures:

> We also had quite lengthy essays to write in Dutch and mine were pretty basic although grammatically correct as I didn't have the breadth of vocab. that the others had. Mine was learnt from a book whereas theirs was learnt at home talking Dutch to their parents.

Here the student is reporting an examination technique which is often used by students. Make the most of what you know and don't be overwhelmed by all that you don't know. However, as we shall see in the final chapter of this book, her technique worked only because she was not penalised for using simple vocabulary and a basic set of structures. That is not always the basis for marking. Some markers reward complex language:

> Yes, I did finally pass but probably with a sympathy pass from the lecturer. Looking back it would have been better if Stage 2 could have been confined to non-Dutch background speakers. Also learning only grammar

was not satisfactory. None of the non-Dutch background speakers could speak fluently at the end of the course. When we had to speak it we all mentally translated and then trotted the sentence out, hoping that the person would not reply.

Here is a question to ask about the course you are enrolling for. Will native speakers of the language be grouped in the same classes as beginners? Again the student comments:

It was a traditional approach to teaching but we were not traditional people. We wanted to speak Dutch rather than read or write it (limited opportunities for that) but we weren't asked what we wanted and being sort of polite people we accepted what we were given. And at the beginning it felt as if this was what we wanted because it was safe and secure but when we realised what we wanted it was too late.

Many courses are already organised before staff meet the students, so it is not possible to alter the content or the pace to suit those who have enrolled. Part-time evening courses (see below) are more likely to be flexible according to the composition of the class. They may have an initial questionnaire to find out what students want:

If I had been given a questionnaire before the course started I think I would have said that I wanted the emphasis to be on spoken Dutch. If you had asked me halfway through Stage 1, I would have said I liked the way the course was running but would have changed my mind back again in Stage 2. Stage 1 didn't do us any favours, however easy it seemed, and we didn't realise until it was too late.

If you are studying at a school or a university you will probably be asked to give feedback to the teachers from time to time. There is some advice on this in Chapter 5.

Distance learning

Going along to an institution to study may not suit you. For people who want to study at home, distance learning may be the answer. If you think of distance learning as running to the letterbox every week looking for envelopes full of lessons then you will be surprised to hear of how these courses now take advantage of technology. Send for pamphlets about as many courses as you can and then compare them for their reputation, their content and other details that are important to you. Here are some points to explore.

1 The source of the programme

It's a good idea to find out the standing of the organisation offering the course. Is it privately or government run? Is it linked with a large institution? If so, is it an institution you have heard of before? How long has it been in operation? Has anyone else heard of it? In particular, ask people who are professionally involved in language teaching. Although they may be reluctant to pass judgement on colleagues, they should be able to give you the factual information you want.

2 Resources

The resources needed to study on a distance-learning course are usually built into the initial cost. However, this is not always the case. Find out what books, tapes or compact disks you will need to provide for yourself. The absolute minimum would probably be a book, but you may also need access to a tape recorder and, for the many computer-based programmes available, a computer of your own. If you have access to one that is linked with the Internet and e-mail then there are further options for courses. Search for one that makes the most of the facilities you already have.

3 Time

Time considerations include the total length of the course as well as the weekly time commitment for study. Are the courses taught at a time when all the students need to be at their computers simultaneously (real time) or can communication happen at a time that suits the learners? Could you access courses offered in parts of the world that are in different time zones from you? Studying in the middle of the night may not worry you.

4 Assessment and qualifications

Many people are happy to study a language without aiming for any form of qualification. If you are not one of those, find out how you will be assessed and whether that way suits you. Will there be a final examination or is the course assessed on the basis of assignments throughout the year? What proportion of the final mark is from each part? Is there an emphasis on oral or on written work? If you want an end-of-course certificate or other qualification, who recognises this institution's programmes? A qualification might have status in some countries or might be recognised by some employers but not others.

5 Contact with other students

You may think that distance learning is a rather solitary and unnatural way to learn a language, which, by definition, involves communication. This is not necessarily the case. For many distance-learning projects you can still be in touch with other students through e-mail if the course organisers provide you with address contacts. They may even organise computer conferencing, when you talk with other learners via your computer.

For non-computer courses students sometimes agree to have their names and telephone numbers given to others so that a 'class' can be in touch with one another that way. There is also the idea of study groups with people who live near you.

6 Contact with tutors

As with a course you attend in person, you will want to have contact with someone who guides and teaches you. Distance learning is not the same as self-study (which we look at next). You can expect with distance learning to have direct contact with one or more tutors. Find out how accessible they are likely to be. When you send in a query, how long could you expect to wait for an answer? How often are you allowed to be in touch? Is it the teachers or the learners or both who initiate contact?

Self-study

If you prefer to study completely independently, with no tutor and no assignments that have to be sent away for assessment, you have three options. You can get hold of some sort of package (usually a book and tapes or a compact disk) in a shop or through mail order; you can look for a programme on the Internet; or you can follow a language course on television or radio. From there, all it takes is determination and some time management. Here are some considerations as you choose your self-study course.

Finishing level

Glance at the last chapter of the course book. Where does this course offer to take you by the last lesson? Is that far enough for you? If not, see whether a second level is available when you finish. On the other hand, beware of miracle claims. The materials are only half the story. Your progress will depend partly on the time you have available to study and partly on other factors such as your own motivation.

Language version

For some languages, such as Chinese and Spanish, there are geographical variations. Make sure you have the version of the tapes and books you want. Also, are the instructions in English?

Cost

Of course, cost applies whichever way you choose to study but beware of paying out more than you need initially for a self-study programme that you may or may not want to finish. See whether you can buy the materials in stages.

Part-time evening courses

People who attend a part-time evening class have many reasons for choosing this option, such as the fact that it is probably the cheapest and the least disruptive to one's working and social life. Because these courses often have to cater for a tremendous range of purposes, not to mention commitment to study, it is worth taking time at the start to find out whether the one that is nearest to you is also the most suitable.

Focus

Ask what the basic aim of the course is. People signing up will have all sorts of reasons for learning, some of which are difficult to deal with in one class. They may be learning the language

As preparation for a short holiday
In order to read professional articles
To learn how to have simple conversations with overseas visitors
To live in the country semi-permanently
For cultural interest
As a hobby to fill lonely evenings.

Materials

Ask to see a sample of the textbook. If there isn't one, and all the learning takes place via teacher-made tapes and handouts, it will be more difficult for you to work ahead should you wish. Everyone in the class will have to learn at the same pace.

Length of course

In some institutions night classes for the public have a low priority and depend on numbers. You might find that the class fades out part-way through the winter if numbers drop.

Private tutors

Some people enjoy working with a private tutor. Although it can be expensive, particularly if your tutor is well qualified, some of that cost might be saved in travel and institutional fees.

The tutor's qualifications and experience

You have probably heard the expression about paying peanuts if you want monkeys. That may not be absolutely fair in relation to private tutors because some people give lessons for the enjoyment of it. However, if you are interested in being taught by someone with qualifications, ask about them. You could also ask about the tutor's experience as a teacher. Qualifications may not bother you but it is certainly not the case that anyone who speaks a language can teach it. If you have a choice between, say, an untrained native speaker and a trained non-native speaker, then you need to know what your priorities are. A native speaker could be ideal if you know exactly how you want to learn and the tutor is willing to follow your suggestions. That should be one of the

big advantages of private tutoring – you have a say in how the lessons
are organised. The last thing you want is a tutor who has a fixed idea
about how to teach a language, if that way does not relate at all to the
way you want to learn. If it's the teaching skills as well as the language
skills that you value, then go for the trained person.

The tutor's time commitment

Try and find out how available the tutor will be as the year goes on.
Tutors who are also university students, for example, may find they have
no time to give lessons as examinations come closer. Newly retired
language teachers could have time available right through the year and
native speakers who are keen for others to learn their language could
also turn out to be generous with their time.

Suggestions for working with a tutor

The first suggestion for studying one-to-one with a private tutor is that
during the lesson the roles should be shared. The tutor sometimes asks
questions and sometimes answers them. The student takes a share in
determining the lesson content and the learning methods. Here are
some specific ways of sharing the planning:

1.   Define the intended outcomes of the course
How far do you want to go in what length of time? Sharing responsibility for setting these general outcomes puts you into an active mode and
reminds the tutor of the seriousness of the lessons. See Chapter 5 for
ideas on goal-setting.

2.   Decide how you plan to get there
Planning includes agreeing on time commitments and deciding on the
books and other resources you will need. It also includes decisions about
how formal or informal you want the lessons to be and what proportion
of time you want to spend on learning new language as opposed to
practising it. If your tutor is a native speaker of the language, do you
also want to use him or her to talk about cultural matters?

3.   Define the course content
Think about the content of the course. Do you want to have general
language, or language for a particular purpose? If, for example, you
want to learn the language because you are involved in an agricultural

project in another country, is it possible to have a tutor with that specialised knowledge?

4. *Agree to review the lessons from time to time*

If your tutor asks broad questions such as whether you are enjoying your lessons, then there is really only one answer that a polite person can give. Plan to ask each other specific questions, such as these:

> Which things are going best at the start of the lesson?
> Which of the activities we have tried have been most helpful?
> Do we still need a text book?
> What other resources could we use?
> What should we do next?

5. *Plan between-lesson activities*

For example, if you have recorded early lessons, you can listen to the recordings again and notice how many more words and sentence patterns you now know.

Living in another country

Many language courses include time when students go and live in a country to try out their skills in a new language and to learn more. Some schools and universities may even give credit for these visits. If not, students can choose to organise this experience for themselves even before they start their language study. The aim is for students to learn by immersing themselves in the language and the culture. The term 'immersion' is used to describe language learning that takes place by the learner living surrounded by native speakers. Motivated students who also have ideas about how to learn in this way can do well as long as they understand that being surrounded by a language does not automatically lead to learning it. Generations of English-speaking people have lived in countries like India, Malaysia and East Africa, to name a few, without ever learning the languages spoken around them.

However, it can work well for someone who is determined. Here is the account of one student who went overseas at the end of her secondary schooling. She chose to live in Costa Rica and Mexico for eighteen months before going to university to study Spanish. She returned for another three months after her first year of study. As we shall see, she combined immersion with a good deal of her own effort. Her experiment was successful and at the time she gave this account she was completing her Master's degree.

The experience of being a beginner

(The numbers throughout her account refer to the notes that follow, which make connections with all the other information that is presented in the first section of this book.)

It was a great way to learn. It was the ultimate in absorbing a language. It amazed me how the brain can absorb things.(1) At first I knew nothing and then gradually I found myself being able to tell what was a question and what was a command or comment just from the inflections and situation.(2) I did that by living with Spanish-speaking people. That speeded up the process. I also made a real effort to try and remember words, asking people to explain things to me. It certainly wasn't all passive absorption.(3)

The best thing about doing it that way round was that I wasn't thinking in translation at all. It was only when I returned to university that I suddenly realised, 'Oh, that's the English word!' While I was in Costa Rica I attended a course for foreign language learners. Even though it wasn't much of a course it did help me with grammar points or at least very basic ones.(4)

Pronunciationwise, being in a Spanish-speaking country was very helpful. I could hear it all the time. Basically it was much less work. The first time I woke and realised I'd been dreaming in Spanish I thought that I really must be in Spanish mode. Being there was also a way of learning the culture at the same time as the language.(5)

There were times of frustration, like the first three months. It was incredibly lonely having nobody to talk to and quite belittling because you have to be dragged around by the hand like a little kid on show. I never knew where we were going until we got there. It's also very tiring. My brain actually felt tired from listening and trying to make sense of the language but you get past that point fairly fast. After three or four months I was understanding quite well and by six months I could express anything I wanted. The other trainees found the same thing except that the ones who had learned a language before were faster. From six months on, it was a question of perfecting things.(6)

After six months I was working in a day care centre, which worked well. Kids talk away to you like a normal person, not changing, the way adults do if they know you are a learner. They also laughed at you, which was a good way of monitoring mistakes. Adults are too polite. They can even freeze up when they realise what your language is like. Other students there on exchange found the same thing.(7)

Anywhere you work you learn different types of specialised vocabulary, so with Amnesty International I tended to learn expressions for refugees, torture and political terms whereas with the children it was more the language of their daily lives. In general I felt I learned vocabulary specific to their language rather than the things I'd be talking about at home.(8)

I actually had to relearn some vocabulary in changing between Costa Rica and Mexico. There seemed to be regional differences. It was quite exciting to be told in Mexico that I spoke Spanish like a Costa Rican. Now at university I've been learning the better known, generic terms.(9)

1. Here the speaker is drawing attention to the difference between conscious and unconscious language learning. In a language class you are usually paying conscious attention to the language, whereas when you are living in another country and mixing with people who speak the language, you are all the time attending to real-life events and absorbing the language less consciously. Of course this difference is not absolute. People in language classes can get caught up in interesting activities too.

2. There are a couple of interesting comments here. One is our need to distinguish between the different functions of language, all of which seem to be just one long rush of speech at the start. The second is the role of intonation in meaning. This role is stronger in some languages than others. As you will know if you are studying a tonal language like Chinese or Vietnamese, even the tone within one word can make a fundamental difference to the meaning.

3. The learner's effort is starting to be obvious here. First there was the effort of putting herself into an environment where she started by knowing absolutely nothing, and then there was the effort of conscious memorising and asking questions.

4. Now there is the even more conscious step of joining a class. Despite the teaching methods not being what she might have wished, she managed to find some purpose in them. Conscious attention to the form of the language was something she wasn't getting in her everyday contacts.

5. Pronunciation and culture are mentioned together here as two things that, unlike new words, cannot be learned within a finite time. The student constantly had models of pronunciation to measure herself against. The culture too made sense as part of everyday life rather than as a list of differences between one culture and another.

6. The emotional aspect of language learning is mentioned by many students. Feelings, positive and negative, are a very important part of language learning. Notice how determined people have to be to isolate themselves from contacts with their own language group, in the interests of speeding up the learning process. Notice too, though, that in a relatively short time, in this case six months, the speaker moved from feeling like a little child to being able to express herself in adult ways. It is wise to be ready for the negative feelings that are bound to be part of the experience of being an adult with only a child's command of the language. Think about how long it takes, and how frustrating it is to be reduced to childhood again.

   When you start to speak a new language, something happens to your identity. If you are an extrovert who enjoys having a go at new things, you may enjoy the sensation of speaking in an entirely different way, while others may feel stupid making strange sounds.

7. Think about who you will talk to and vice versa. For this student, children turned out to be a great source of language input. Other learners have spoken of having landladies, or elderly relatives of the families where they were staying, as good informants.

8. Plan a context for learning. What exactly will you do all day as you learn the language? Joining in regular activities with people you would want to communicate with anyway is a great idea if you can manage it. For example, you may be able to work in the country or even attend classes that have nothing officially to do with language learning, such as Japanese flower arranging. This student's account is a good example of learning the language needed immediately instead of learning predetermined lists of words from a textbook and then hoping for chances to use them. When you are selecting the work you want to do, if you have a choice, think about areas of language you would like to be fluent in.

   It also pays to find out about the wider context of the country where you plan to live. What do you know about living conditions? Is it easy to make arrangements for living and working or studying? Can you find out anything about the people's attitude to foreigners? Will you see it as an advantage or not if there are no people there who can speak your own language? How will you get by for communication in the time before you start to express yourself? Will you be able to get hold of learning resources like dictionaries and reference books if you want them?

9. Finally, the student mentions the best aspects of both informal and formal learning. The story seems to be this. Make the most of the class learning but remember to keep trying out your new language in real contexts.

SUMMARY OF ADVICE

Here is a summary of advice you could follow if you are starting out in your language studies.

1. Having a reason for learning a language is a strong motivation to work hard at it.

2. There is hardly a language in the world that has not been learned by some foreigner. You can do it!

3. There is no such thing as a best course. Choose one that suits you. Advice about particular courses has to be taken carefully because what suits one learner may not suit another.

5. If, in the end, you wish you had chosen another language, remember that learning one language makes it easier to learn the next one.

NOTE

1. Metalanguage = the words used to describe language. See the last section of Chapter 2.

2

KNOWING A LANGUAGE: WHAT DOES IT MEAN?

People talk admiringly about how many languages others know but when they talk about their own language knowledge they are more conservative. They realise that there is much more to knowing a language than being able to exchange short conversations with visiting tourists. This chapter investigates four aspects involved in 'knowing' a language.

What does it mean to know a language? For the moment let's compare it with learning to ride a bicycle. When you learned that skill as a child there were at least three things involved. You needed some actual information, such as how the brakes worked. Then there were the skills, such as not losing your balance. The third part had to do with your attitude, especially when you felt you were not making progress. In both riding a bicycle and learning a language you are building on what has gone before, whether that was keeping your balance while riding a tricycle or climbing a tree or, in the case of languages, speaking and understanding your own language already.

What do you actually need to know? The knowledge you need can be summarised under these headings:

Knowledge about the form of the language
Knowledge about how the language is used in different situations
Knowledge about putting the language together in speech and writing
Words to describe what you know

According to one student, some courses concentrate mainly on the form of the language (pronouncing and spelling words properly), forgetting that the social rules are important. So, too, is the business of making sure what you say or write fits in with everything else that is being said and written. What he says about learning Japanese could just as easily be said about learning other languages:

> I think the other thing people should be careful of when studying Japanese is not to fall into the trap of thinking that learning lots of vocab. or grammar structures is the be all, although they are of course essential. I found that there was very little concentration on my part, and on the part of teachers, on discourse-level competence [the way ideas are joined together in speech and writing]. Sociolinguistic competence is not covered enough at Uni either. The way for learners to combat this problem is to make Japanese friends and talk with them, and more importantly, listening to their speech. There are heaps of Japanese coming to this country to visit for working holidays, etc., all the time, and a lot of them are pretty hopeless at English, so there is no shortage of subjects!!

We look now at each of these aspects in turn.

2.1 THE FORM OF THE LANGUAGE

The information you learned about a bicycle's parts was probably quite simple. You knew there were wheels to keep you moving, brakes to stop you, and handlebars to hold on to in the meantime.

Before you ever started formal foreign-language learning you probably had an impression about languages other than your own. People pick up bits of folk information such as these:

German has very long words.
Chinese uses tones.
Some languages use polite language for talking to certain people.

For some years, knowing *about* our own language has been seen as not very important. Language learners would often be able to describe another language better than their own. This viewpoint has changed a little. Whereas we learn our first language as babies and little children, a language studied at high school or university is studied more consciously. Students don't have all those years to spend on their learning and they find that actually making conscious some of the knowledge that's unconscious in relation to their own language speeds the process up.

In Chapter 10 there are suggestions for learning grammar. In this section we are considering what grammar actually is. Try yourself out with this question. When you hear the word grammar what do you picture? Is it the way small words are added to a phrase to change meaning? Is it the rules about putting sentences together? Over the years the word grammar has expanded to include the way a language's sound system works, the way its words are put together, and the bigger picture, the way sentences and longer units of meaning are put together.

Here is a suggested summary of what people need to know about a new language. If you are a student of linguistics as well as of languages, you will know it already.

Patterns of sound

One of the most striking things you will notice about the language you are learning is its sound. Each language has its own distinctive sounds, including its patterns of word stress and intonation. Some people claim they can listen to voices through a closed door and know what language is being spoken on the other side just from the intonation patterns.

You learn these patterns more by listening than by reading books of rules. Gradually you start to use the new sounds yourself. There are chapters on learning to listen and learning to speak in the second half of this book. For the moment, here are some of the things you can start listening for in the language you are learning.

Distinctions that affect meaning

In every language there are sounds that make a difference to meaning and sounds that don't. In English, for instance, it matters whether you say to your fellow students, 'Have you seen my tie?' or 'Have you seen my dye?' but in some languages the distinction between /t/ and /d/ is not important. Sometimes the sound takes one form and sometimes another, but there are no words where the meaning depends on hearing that difference. An English example of this is the way we say the letter /l/. Your tongue can be in all sorts of positions in your mouth when you say it, depending on the sounds that went before and the sounds that follow, but we still think of it as an /l/.

Think about the language you are learning. Are there some pairs of sounds that you have to distinguish that are not important in English?

Many native speakers of English find it very hard at first to hear a difference between the different tones, in Chinese for example, and even when they can hear it they don't find it easy to use the right tone at the right time.

The pattern of syllables

Another difference you may notice between the sound of the two languages, the one you know and the one you are learning, has to do with the way syllables are put together. What sort of letters start syllables and how can syllables finish? You may find that a sound you make very easily in one place in a word seems difficult somewhere else. English-speaking New Zealanders, for instance, have no trouble saying words like sing, bring, looking and thinking, but when they try to say Maori words that start with *ng* like *nga*, they find it feels awkward at first.

Here's another difference in syllables. Does the language you are learning have plenty of clusters of consonants as in the English words *split* and *ankle* or are its consonants always separated by vowels? These are just some of the differences your ear and your tongue will have to become accustomed to.

Stress and intonation

As well as the individual sounds and syllables, you have to know about word stress in the new language. If you are fortunate, the language you are learning will have some clear patterns. If not, then every time you learn a word you must be quite clear in your mind where the stress falls. In English there are patterns, but not everything fits them. Try pronouncing these two:

below   bellow

The effect of not getting the stress and intonation patterns right ranges from being misunderstood to being understood but sounding odd.

Patterns in words

It's one thing to know lists and lists of words but you also need to reflect on the lists. Language students are often not as good at that as they might be. They write out lists, stick them on the bathroom mirror, they use highlighters to emphasise groups of words and so on. Having a range of words is, of course, at the heart of language learning, as we'll see in Chapter 7.

Word formation

The more you know about how words are formed, the speedier your learning. Instead of memorising each word separately you start to notice patterns. You notice, perhaps, that nouns and verbs are identified by their endings or, if you are learning a language with characters, you notice that knowing small units of meaning can help you to understand new and more complicated characters.

Take, for example, the Japanese word for 'rock' or 'rocky cliff', which in the Kanji form looks like Figure 2.1. The top part of the symbol is the word for mountain; the lower part means stone, so that together they mean a rocky cliff. Once you know that, you will be able to understand many other words made up of those parts.

FIGURE 2.1

Phrase formation

The fixed phrases of the language are the groups of words which have a meaning of their own beyond the meaning of the individual words in them. In English, for example, native speakers know the difference between putting someone down, putting them up, putting them off and so on, but these multiple meanings are a nightmare for the language learner. Every language has its common phrases. Start to note what some of these are in the language you are studying. Some examples are:

Greetings and farewells,
Apologies,

Thanks,
Asking people to make themselves clearer,
Linking your comment with the last person's.

Sentence patterns

The next level of language knowledge relates to the way words are put together in sentences or utterances. We use the word utterances because of course when people speak they do not always speak in traditional sentences. Together these rules make up what is called the syntax of a language.

In many languages, including English and other European languages, word order plays a big part in meaning. In the sentence 'Man bites dog,' we know who did the biting because of the word order. Change the order of the two nouns around and the man will be suffering the injuries. As well as word order there are all the ways in which one language expresses key ideas like time, space, amount and so on. Time is expressed through

Word endings (*I screamed*, *I was screaming*),
Words and phrases (*yesterday*, *in a minute*, *long ago*),
The order of writing events in a text (I came. I saw. I conquered.).

Some ideas that are important in one language are less important in another. English, for instance, expresses the difference between definite and indefinite both in the singular (*a dog*, *the dog*) and in the plural (*dogs*, *the dogs*). In other languages the definite/indefinite distinction is not at all important.

Longer patterns of text

Just to state the obvious, the language you are learning is made up of thousands of words linked in various ways. People used to pay attention mainly to the grammar of sentences but now there is emphasis on knowing how huge chunks of text, either spoken or written, are put together. The shape of a huge piece of text is affected by different rules in different cultures.

As you become more advanced in your language and want to write connected prose, fiction or non-fiction, you will learn a variety of phrases. The same applies to making a speech or even to taking part in conversations. In your reading you can start to note phrases that link ideas. In the following, phrases are given in brackets.

> Cause and effect (*as a result of*)
> Making things clear (*in other words*)
> Conceding a point (*even though*)
> Qualifying a statement (*as far as we know*)
> Making a different or opposing point (*on the other hand*)
> Linking through time (*some time later*)
> Summarising (*in a word*).

The emphasis now in language learning is that you should find out how to use language to express the meaning you want. The more you know about the form of the language you are studying, the better you are able to express detailed meaning, because grammar is only a means to an end. Many people are fascinated by the topic of language description and they want to read more about it. If you are one of those, then look for a simple introduction to linguistics such as those listed at the end of the book.

Only some words are directly transferrable from one language to another. These are usually the words that take up a huge proportion of language textbooks, perhaps because they are so easily illustrated (*chair*, *table*, *mountain*, *train* and so on). It is easy to forget that what you think of as a mountain, a native speaker may consider a hill.

Another point to know is that a great deal of the meaning in languages comes through the little words that have many different meanings. In English, prepositions are a good example of this. Think of the different uses of the little word in: in time, in a hurry, in Portugal, in springtime, in case, all in all.

2.2   LANGUAGE USE IN DIFFERENT SITUATIONS

Another aspect that you need to know about your new language is what differences there are (and how firm they are) in the language used for different situations. In some languages such as French and German different forms of address show different relationships between speakers. Whether you use 'tu' or 'vous', 'du' or 'Sie' (to express the English concept of *you*) depends on a number of factors. Here are some questions to try answering for the language you are learning.

> What are the main differences between spoken and written language?
> Can there be formal and informal language in both speech and writing?
> What are some of the distinctions that count (age, friend/stranger, status in society)?
> Are these differences at the level of vocabulary, structures, idioms, topics?

Spoken and written language

Here are some of the differences to keep in mind between written and spoken language.

Meaning that comes from the context

In speech the context helps in making sense of what people are saying. This can be a trap when you are talking to people who have a different background from yours. It is easy to assume that everyone knows what you mean. In writing, on the other hand, people spell things out more. Instead of using phrases such as 'like this' or 'over there' they substitute words that have meaning.

Complexity

Contrary to popular belief, both speech and writing can be very informal or very formal.

Solo or cooperative language use

Another obvious difference between speech and writing is that when you speak you are usually sharing communication time. The exception is when you are giving a formal presentation or speech, which is sometimes easier, because all you have to think about is your own words and ideas. It's much easier to plan something you want to say, say it and then stop talking, but that's not taking part in a conversation.

In writing there is less cooperation. You send away a written message and the other person can ignore it or take time to answer.

Time to think

That leads to another difference between speech and writing, which is the opportunity to plan and modify your language. You can plan more easily in writing than in speech. What you have said is heard by everyone, even if you try and patch up misunderstandings later.

Sentences and non-sentences

Then there is the question of what is and is not a sentence. Whereas in writing, languages tend to be used in traditional units called sentences, in speech, as you know from your own language, people meander on, joining up ideas or not joining them, in a less organised way.

Cultural values

Finally, there is the question of different attitudes towards speech and writing. Any of the following attitudes towards speech and writing could exist in the culture whose language you are learning.

1. Formal speeches are as important as written documents.
2. People should think before they write but they can say whatever they like (or vice versa).
3. Chunks of written language are memorised and recited aloud for entertainment.
4. Only very educated people learn formal writing.

A little language goes a long way

Every piece of language you utter has a purpose to it, whether that purpose is to sound annoyed or to ask for something. As your language skills develop you will be able to do in the foreign language more and more of the things you can do in your own: criticising or praising, accepting or refusing. How the criticism or praise is expressed differs from one language to another, as we'll see in Chapter 14 on 'Culture and Language Learning'.

Learning a language communicatively means being interested in the purposes you can use it for, and here is the good news. One grammatical structure can have many purposes. If you say to someone, 'I'm having a party on Saturday night,' that can be an invitation or a piece of information. It could even be a threat if you are warning adults in the house to keep away.

At the early stages of your language learning you are probably wishing you had more sophisticated language to use but if you can make the little you do have work for many different purposes, you could feel less frustrated.

2.3 PUTTING LANGUAGE TOGETHER

Linking ideas

So far we have considered the form of the language: sounds, words and sentences. Now we look at keeping the language flow going, whether in speech or in writing.

The language of conversations

In the late 1960s and early 1970s one way of learning a language was to memorise as many dialogues as possible. The idea was that knowing how chunks of language are put together gave the learner a start in conversations. The good thing about this technique was that people learned standard ways for following on from one speaker to the next. There were problems though. One was that unless you talked only to other students using the same textbook, you found yourself waiting for a response that didn't come. Beyond the classroom, the other speaker not only had original ideas, but also had original language to express them in.

To be good at conversation, the language learner has to know certain strategies for staying afloat when all around you is a sea of noise. More information on general communication strategies follows in the next chapter, and on strategies for speaking in Chapter 9.

The language of writing

Writing in a new language means much more than translating or doing exercises from a textbook. Depending on how far you take your language studies, you could, as in your first language, want to write everything from informal messages on the e-mail to creative writing. Each type has its own conventions, as we shall see in Chapter 13.

2.4 DESCRIBING LANGUAGE

We have talked so far in this chapter about the sort of language knowledge that helps you use language. In this final section we'll consider how to describe the language you are learning. Knowing the language and knowing how to describe it are not the same thing. It is possible to describe a language in some detail without actually understanding or using it. Conversely, millions of people use a language, their own included, but can't answer questions like 'What's the difference between expressing doubt and certainty in your language?' In old-fashioned terms, answering this question means being able to label a language grammatically, knowing words *about* language rather than words *in* the language. Here are three questions to consider about describing language.

First, do you want or need to learn grammatical labels? If not, head straight for the next chapter. In some courses, particularly in the first year or two of learning a language, teachers and textbooks pay no attention to language description. If your course is one of these, then the only point in going beyond the course and learning the labels for yourself is because you are interested or think it will help you. For example, if you have already learned grammatical terms in your own language or another, then it will probably help you to do the same thing in the new language.

A second question is whether you prefer to learn these labels in your own language or in the one you are learning. In the early stages the most common practice is to use your own language. There are enough new terms to master without that additional burden. Even quite advanced grammar books for learners of a particular language will use terms and explanations in the mother tongue. On the other hand, if you are an advanced student or if you plan to study in the country where the language is used, then learning the grammatical terms in the new language makes sense.

Thirdly, there is the question of which grammar labels to learn. There are traditional and functional labels. We'll see now what each of those means, taking examples from textbooks for learning many different languages.

Traditional grammar labels

You may choose to skip this section, either because you already know the terms or because you are more interested in functional grammar. Traditional grammar labels include categories into which words or phrases can be put, and all the exceptions to these categories. For instance, in English the word *noun* is used to describe labels for people (*soldiers*, *leaders*, *a baby*), places (*the park*, *Beijing*, *houses*), things and ideas (*hamburgers*, *greed*, *a plan*), while the word *pronoun* describes all those little words that stand for nouns (*he*, *them*, *her*) and which don't make sense unless you know the context.

Adjectives (*large*, *blue*, *difficult*) add meaning to nouns. Depending on the language you are learning they will be placed either before the noun as in English (*huge debts*), or after the noun, or as some other part of the sentence.

Prepositions (*above*, *below*, *near*) show relationships, and *adverbs* (*now*, *quickly*, *very*) add meaning to other words. In terms of meaning, a sentence like 'He told them about it,' being full of pronouns (*he*, *her*, *it*), tells you absolutely nothing about what happened if it is said in isolation, whereas the sentence 'The captain told the telegraphists about the water pouring into the hold,' being full of nouns, conjures up a picture even for someone who hasn't heard the rest of the story.

Each of these categories can be further subdivided. We talk about *concrete nouns* (*flower*, *bicycle*, *water*) for things you can touch, smell, taste, hear or see, and *abstract nouns* (*idea*, *fear*, *courage*). Of course some nouns could be used in both ways on different occasions and some nouns can be combined with various forms of punctuation in different languages. We call these combinations *compound nouns*, as in *goal post*, *war zone*, *fruit stall*.

Articles (*a*, *an*, *the*) are another part of speech that can be tricky between languages. As we have noted, some have them, some don't. In English, we call the first two (*a*, *and*) the *indefinite articles* because the speaker is not being definite about what he is referring to. Thus in the sentence 'I saw a dog as I tried to get past your front gate,' the speaker is deliberately vague about what kind of dog it was and whether it was yours. He may know or he may not know but the intention is to be vague. On the other hand 'I saw the dog as I tried to get past your front gate' uses the *definite article* in front of 'dog'. Here the assumption is that speaker and listeners all know which dog is being referred to. It could be the one next door that everyone is afraid of or it could be yours but in that subtle change from the indefinite to the definite article a different message has been given. To make things more complicated, the plural of the indefinite is nothing (I saw dogs) while the plural of the definite remains the same (I saw the dogs). If you are learning a language that either has the same use of articles as English or doesn't use articles at all, your only concern will be which to use when you translate into English.

Verbs are usually described as expressing actions (*jump*, *run*) or states (*are*, *become*) but many other words that don't seem to fall neatly under those labels are also verbs (*have*, *think*). One of the trickiest aspects of labelling verbs comes when you get past the form that is listed as the main dictionary item (usually called the *infinitive*, as in *to run*) and on to the various parts that indicate how many people did the thing (he runs) and when (she ran). These labels vary according to the language you are learning but in many cases they refer to time (past, present, future, and further subdivisions).

Adverbs, as their name suggests, add meaning to verbs. Examples of adverbs in English are *fast*, *slowly*, *indiscriminately* and *well*.

Exclamations are the words we use to indicate emotions, either positive (Great! Congratulations!), negative (Stop! Wait!) or neutral (Oh!).

The clue to the meaning of another part of speech, *prepositions*, is in the second half of the word. These usually small words (*in*, *on*, *under*, *around*) refer to the position of things, either literally as in 'on the moon' or figuratively as in 'under consideration'.

For *numerals* there is a distinction to make in some languages between the *cardinals* (*one*, *two*, *three*) and the *ordinals* (*first*, *second*, *third*), which, to state the obvious, tell you the order.

As well as all these parts of speech there are words to describe the role a particular word or group of words plays in a sentence. There is a lot more to be said on this topic, but for this purpose we'll start by describing *subjects* and two kinds of *objects*. In the sentence

You give him the horse and he'll bring it back

we have a couple of *subjects* (*you/he*), a couple of *direct objects* (*the horse/it*) and one *indirect object* (*him*).

At a bigger level, we refer to groups of words that belong together as *phrases*, and even longer groups as *sentences*. In the following sentence we can identify three phrases:

[*After months of hardship*] they crawled [*out of the jungle*] [*calling for help*.]

That sentence has a subject (*they*) but no direct object. The following sentence does have a direct object.

They said they'd eaten *berries* to keep alive.

When it comes to describing sentence types in traditional grammar terms we talk about *statements, questions, commands* and *exclamations*. Here is an example of each.

> *I'll eat that.* (statement)
> *Will he eat that?* (question)
> *Eat it up.* (command)
> *Yuck!* (exclamation)

The difference between sentence types could be created by word order, by the words themselves, by the use of punctuation and, in spoken language, by intonation.

Other languages will have different grammatical items which are important. For example, in Vietnamese there is a final *particle* that can be added to an interrogative sentence to call for someone's sympathy with the speaker's action.

As you will know from any language study you have done, the whole of language is not divided neatly into sentences. People use plenty of shorter utterances when they are speaking and writing. This problem with labelling is partly overcome if you use functional grammar. Labelling various utterances in functional grammar depends on knowing why someone has said something. We'll look now at functional labels.

Functional grammar labels

Most textbooks now use functional terms, or at least a mixture of traditional and functional, as the main basis for organising grammar points. The point of functional grammar is to answer the question: Why did this person use these words? Unlike most of the terms used in traditional grammar, the same words can be labelled differently according to the user's intentions. A more complex question is whether the speaker/listener and reader/writer understand the same intention as each other. That's a topic for your linguistics book.

Here are some functional grammar labels taken from recent textbooks. Examples have been added in English, but of course you would need to know the context to be really sure of the speaker's intention.

Imparting and seeking factual information
   You can have a free coffee if you buy two hamburgers.
   What do I get if I don't like coffee?

Expressing and finding out attitudes
   What did you think of that fantastic movie?
   I can't agree with the word 'fantastic'.
   If there's one thing I can't stand it's hypocrisy.
   Who likes watching football?
   I'm really sorry about that.
   I couldn't care less.

Getting things done
   Give us a hand, will you?
   Everyone line up over here.
   You are invited to our 70th wedding anniversary.

Socialising
   It's good to see you.
   How's your cat?
   See you later.

When you are learning another language it is not just a case of finding out how they say such-and-such in their language. It is also a question of knowing whether they say it at all.

What else do language students need to know?

This chapter has discussed what you need to know about the language you are learning: the form of the language, its use in different situations and the language for talking about language. The next chapter addresses the question: 'What do students need to know about the learning process?' starting with information about strategies for better learning and then moving to the topic of motivation.

3

LANGUAGE LEARNING: COMPARISONS AND CONTRASTS

We know a great deal about the language-learning process, but individual learners still have a large part to play in making their learning successful. Successful learners are people who choose useful ways to study. They also manage to use the language they do know to compensate for all the language they still have to learn. You may think that teachers or lecturers are the ones who decide how you will learn, but this chapter suggests decisions you can make for yourself.

One interesting discovery by researchers studying the language-learning process is that what students believe about the learning process makes a difference to their learning, whether or not their beliefs are held by other learners, by teachers and by researchers. The first half of this chapter addresses three frequently asked questions about language learning in relation to first and second languages. In the second half we consider individual differences in the learning process. Finally we review strategies used by successful language learners.

3.1 FIRST- AND SECOND-LANGUAGE LEARNING

The general points in this section refer to whatever language is being learned, although English is used as an illustration here and throughout the book.

How do children learn a first language?

When we talk about learning we include understanding and using language, which highlights one thing about first-language learning as a child – the time available for listening before speaking. There are months and months of gradual understanding before a baby responds in a way that most of us would label language. During all of that time, meaning has been central to every action and every bit of language.

Unlike adults, children are happy to experiment with bits of language they hear. They will talk and talk with all sorts of incomplete, extraneous and unclear sounds. The meaning of what they are saying will sometimes come as a result of whatever response they get from using that bit of language. A good example of that could be the word *'please'* in English, which is the basis of campaigns for politeness by some parents. It may well be that a child uses the word in the same way as a parrot learns to say something that brings food when wanted. Gradually the word becomes associated with asking and even persuading people to give the child what he or she wants.

This use of *'please'* is also an example of imitation. Children will say a thing over and over again often in meaningful ways and sometimes as babble. In return they often get back a range of input since adults get tired of saying the same thing in the same way. A child who announces ten times through the evening 'gone sleep' in relation to a doll she has put to bed will hear answers like these: 'Has she? Let's see. That's good. Goodnight dolly,' and finally perhaps, 'Why don't you go too?' This range of input goes on in a child's life all its waking hours, especially if it has a parent's individual attention. Eavesdropping on a conversation between quite a tiny baby and its parent, you will hear lengthy conversations in which one party makes a string of gurgles and the other carries on as if the gurgles had been perfectly comprehensible.

When children imitate they don't do it word for word. There is a long period of time before parents start to worry about their children's command of the structures of a language. Children use a simplified grammar which becomes more and more complex, but correction seems to make no difference. This applies to the grammar of structures and of sounds. Everyone has an anecdote about children who can distinguish points of pronunciation but not imitate them, as in the following telephone conversation in which the adult imitated the four-year-old child's pronunciation of his own name.

Relative: Hello Gawuff.
Gareth: I'm not Gawuff. I'm Gawuff.

Imitation is particularly easy to observe in relation to intonation. Just before a child starts to use actual words you will notice utterances coming out that are full of expressive intonation patterns that express surprise, enquiries, annoyance and the usual pleading.

When adults address children they usually use some form of modification of their language, which makes the message easy to follow. You can tell people who are unaccustomed to being near children because they fail to make the right modifications or, more humiliating for the child, they overcompensate in relation to the child's age. Children who are slightly older, on the other hand, seem to have a natural ability to modify their language so they can be understood by younger siblings.

All through the pre-school years the child's vocabulary and command of sentence structures are growing. It could take six years of life before a child has more than 2,000 words, although exact numbers vary according to what are counted as separate words.

Can I learn a language like a child?

In some respects you wouldn't want to be learning your second language the way you learned your first as a child. In other ways you might want to be childlike but it simply isn't possible. If you want to be more childlike in your language learning then you will have to decide which features of children's language learning are helpful and possible.

Making sounds

You would probably feel stupid babbling sounds back at an adult in the hope that he would give you back some meaningful answers. Also, because your own physical development is complete you have the ability to make sounds that are difficult for little children even in their own language.

Inhibitions

Adults make slower progress because they are more inhibited. They are more worried about how they sound than about getting their message across in the best way possible. They are also less spontaneous, tending to think before they speak. There are suggestions in this book for trying to put these inhibitions behind you. Adults are also more anxious in general about their progress. You don't often hear little children complaining about not having a sophisticated range of words to use.

Time available

Children have more time at their disposal. The whole of their day, minus sleeping, could be described as one long language lesson. Few adults want to wait six years to reach that 2,000 word total. You took about five years absorbing your first language before there were any serious demands on you to read and write. Do you have that sort of time available for your foreign-language studies? Then there is the question of repetition. As an adult you cannot expect people to talk to you in the repetitious way they do to children. They are likely to tell you things once (twice if you say 'I beg your pardon?') and then move on. Another difference between learning language as a child and as an adult is that almost everything for children is about the here and now and the person, whereas adults want to go further.

Linked with the time factor is repetition, which, as we have seen, children are good at. Young children will say the same thing many times without tiring, whereas most adults move on quickly from one topic to the next. This is something that language learners can arrange for themselves. Thanks to tape-recorders they can not only say the same thing as often as they like but they can also play back their language and listen to it critically.

Amount and type of language input

Another aspect of children's language development is that they usually have more opportunities not only to speak but also to listen than adults do. Because they chatter all the time, with very few silent periods, they also have more input. If you can find people who are very talkative and put yourself in their company then you too will have extra chances for using the language. The more you talk, the more others talk to you, the more language you hear. There are further suggestions in Part II of this book for increasing the input.

Then there is the question of context. Children's language always has a very visible context. In other words they are talking about things they can see and hear, things they are doing. They give running commentaries on their actions. Think of all the games they play where you can see things happen. Without reverting to playing games you might be able to think of activities where the topic is at hand, such as building objects together.

Order of learning

Children seem to learn their own language in a particular order, with all children from one language group tending to follow that order more or less. They learn certain sounds before others, they learn to ask for things before they learn to ask if the people around them would like some. The question sometimes asked is whether adults also acquire a new language in a certain order. Studies provide different answers, because of course many adults learn in classes where the order is decided for them. Others learn from living in the country where the language is used, and they learn according to need.

Some adults say they want their learning organised in order of difficulty, but it is not possible to compare the way a child learns to make sounds with an adult's way of learning. For one thing, physically, certain development has already taken place. Others, especially those who have opportunities to use the language with native speakers, want to start with language that is useful to them immediately. A third group prefer to be driven by topics. If they have an interest in learning language for a particular purpose, such as wanting to read scientific material in German, they may want their language items organised according to topics.

What advantages do adults have?

It may sound as if children have all the advantages. For adults the big advantage is that they know what they are doing and can modify their behaviour accordingly. They are not at the whim of bigger people who can impose language on them, trying to dictate topics. The first advantage of being a mature language learner, then, is your ability to think about the process. You know more about language in general, about the fact that meaning is expressed through intonation and body language. You know, for example, that politeness and rudeness, anger and sadness are universal qualities but that different languages express them in different ways.

Unlike a young child you are able to reason abstractly. You can make a conscious effort to improve in your learning processes as well as in your language. You can stand aside from the process from time to time and measure it. In their bleakest moments some students think, 'It's all too late. I should have learned as a child and now there's no hope.' The question of age comes down to a more specific question: the right age for what aspect of language learning?

It does seem that the younger people are when they learn a foreign language the easier it is for them to have a native-speaker accent. If you have passed childhood it is harder, but not impossible to reach this goal. On the other hand it is worth considering whether you really want to lose your own accent. Accents are part of our identity. If you move from Scotland to England to study, do you really want to change your accent? Why not think of yourself as an English person (or Canadian, or whatever you consider yourself) who is able to speak Russian but remains forever Canadian? Many adults prefer to retain their own accent as part of their identity. The big question is whether they can be understood.

Younger learners do seem to go ahead faster at the basic communication level. They very quickly reach the point where they can chat away to anyone on the subjects that interest children. You are not a child and you want to talk about more sophisticated topics. That is part of the reason why it takes you longer to acquire the language you want. If you were happy to talk all day about the here and now you too could make fast progress.

To sum up the distinctions, it seems that younger is faster for foreign-language learning but older is better in terms of ultimate attainment.

3.2 ABILITY AND METHOD

Are some people more gifted than others for languages?

Students who think that only clever people can learn languages are wrong. In the 1940s and 50s a number of tests were developed to measure aptitude for language learning. They were originally used to screen candidates for foreign-language instruction at the Foreign Service Institute in the United States and then later for placing children in foreign-language programmes in primary schools. Since then other tests have been developed, one of the latest being in the 1970s.

However, interest in aptitude tests has largely faded away. For one thing, they often focused just on the first stages of language development, when people became fluent in conversational language. Another reason why people have lost interest in them is that so many people of all educational levels have become successful sencod-language learners. Researchers have found that innate ability is only one tiny part of the jigsaw of successful language learning. Other factors such as whether or not you have already learned a second language come into play. On the other hand, some people believe that aptitude for language is at the heart of general intelligence.

How important is the teacher's method?

Some students believe that the teacher's methods make all the difference to their progress, especially when these do not coincide with what they believe to be good language-learning processes. For example, if someone has already been successful in learning another language using one method, then he or she may resist efforts by teachers to introduce new ways. For example, perhaps you believe that memorising rules and vocabulary lists is the main learning technique available but the teacher discourages this. Perhaps you want clear and explicit teaching about grammar and vocabulary while your teacher believes that discovering language patterns leads to better understanding.

Conversely, if the earlier method has not led to success then the student is likely to overlook all the other possible reasons for failure and blame the method, even with a different teacher and different materials. They want to try something completely different.

The fact is that throughout the centuries people have learned languages in all sorts of ways. Even in the second part of the twentieth century there have been many, many suggestions for improving language teaching and learning. Here is a brief list of some of the methods, because many people believe that learners should have a chance to select what suits them best from all that is available.

Translation

Translation is now seen as a discipline in its own right. When you have completed a degree in languages, studying to be an interpreter or translator is one of your career options. Translating as a means of language learning is preparation for this and until about the 1960s was the backbone of the language lesson. Many students still say that translation helps them to think in detail about the meaning of language and how different language speakers draw on different imagery to explain their message. There is more on the topic of translation under examination conditions in Chapter 15.

Interpreting is not as common in general language examinations. It is usually taught, along with translating, as part of a professional qualification. It involves putting another person's words into another language, either simultaneously or consecutively. In simultaneous interpreting you are giving out the speaker's message with probably no more than a ten-second delay and with no chance to ask clarifying questions. The audience, or the part of it that needs your interpreting, will hear only your words.

Repetition

Repeating chunks of language has always been the way people learned languages in huge classes, particularly when there were no textbooks. Repetition as a means of language learning had a boost in many countries in the 1960s when tape-recorders became widely available. Language departments had language laboratories where students could spend as long as they wished repeating words, phrases and sentences as a means of remembering and perfecting pronunciation.

There is nothing to stop you from organising your own endless repetition with all the materials available, but you need to keep in mind what is now known about learning new techniques (such as difficult sounds) and about memory. There is more on the topic of memory later in this chapter but, briefly, the message now is that meaningful repetition works well but repetition of bits of language taken out of context doesn't.

Audio-visual language learning

The essence of audio-visual language learning is that you associate sights and sounds with the language in use. The current equivalent is making use of videos and computer-based programmes for language learning. These are probably easily available in your language department and, as many students report, they are a relaxed way of flooding yourself with meaningful language.

Immersion

Although the term 'immersion' is relatively new, the idea is not. Immersion means that you learn the language by plunging yourself totally into the language environment. This usually means living in the country where it is spoken (see Chapter 1) but it can also be done on a more modest scale by spending periods of time with people who speak only the language you want to learn while you are in their company. Of course, there is nothing to stop you from using this technique along with studying in a formal course.

Suggestopedia

In the 1970s an approach to language learning was suggested in which learners were made ready to learn a language in a number of ways such as listening to classical music while reading, or making sure that they were studying in a comfortable place. Many students in our survey reported using music in the background.

Communicative language learning

Communicative language learning cannot be called a method. It is a broad approach which now embraces almost all the language teaching and learning that happens around the world. Learning a language communicatively means that you are constantly getting your examples and practising using language by means of what someone wants to say or write to others. Writing is an important part of communication, and there are many ways in which you can think of your reading as communication (see Chapter 11).

Do learning styles make a difference?

Another question is about learning styles. Do you know what kind of learner you are? From time to time people describe different types of learners and how they study. First we need to distinguish between learning strategies, which everyone can do something about, and learning styles, which are said to reflect differences in our personalities and basic learning preferences. Learning strategies are dealt with later in this chapter, but for the moment let's review what has been said about learning styles. These descriptions are used in general education but have also been applied to language learning.

In the Western world the work of Jung in the 1920s has become well known and has developed in many ways that Jung probably never imagined. He suggested a psychological typology in which there are two typical attitudes in human personalities: *introversion* and *extroversion*. Under these two general types he then said that there are also two perception functions, *intuition* and *sensing*, and two judgement functions, *thinking* and *feeling*. By combining these he came up with eight groupings to describe the personality of individuals, ranging from introvert–intuitive–thinking to extrovert–sensing–feeling.

It is easy to see how some of these traits could apply to specific aspects of language learning, describing what students focus on, and how, during learning. Since Jung's work, language teachers, amongst others, have used and developed his categories to describe individual differences in the way people learn or acquire a second language. The following very brief checklists do not do justice to Jung's work or anyone else's but they could whet your appetite to read more. See how many features of each category seem most like your style.

The analytical language learner

People who like analysing things in the rest of their lives will probably enjoy doing the same thing with language.

1. Can you look at a chunk of text and see connections with any other language you already know?
2. Do you enjoy checking your learning goals from time to time so as to measure your progress?

The concrete language learner

The term 'concrete' has been used to describe people who see language very much as belonging in a context.

1. Do you enjoy using your intuition about how to say something?
2. Using this intuition are you happy to plough ahead in a conversation without paying too much attention to correctness?
   (In return you'll find people speaking back to you a lot.)

The visual learner

Visual learners enjoy anything that supplies graphic support for language learning.

1. Do you make plenty of use of videos and illustrated computer programs?
2. Are your notes arranged graphically?
   (For instance, you experiment with interesting ways of setting out vocabulary items to show the relationship between them.)
3. Do you make and colour mindmaps?
4. Do you use highlighters on your class handouts for a variety of purposes?
5. Are your vocabulary lists full of picture cues?
6. Can you picture a scene while you are listening to audiotapes with your eyes closed?
7. Can you make visual associations between new language and familiar places?
   (For example, for the characters in Chinese and Japanese, you find it easy to picture the roof, trees and the sun in all sorts of words, thus learning their meanings via the original images on which they are based.)

The auditory learner

Sound is important for auditory learners and of course in language learning sound has to be important for everyone. You have to hear the sounds of the new language, individually and in their overall patterns, in order to make the sounds effectively yourself.

1. Do you make plenty of use of audiotapes?
2. Do you wear headphones as you go for a run?
3. Is music an important part of your language study?
4. Do you enjoy selecting and singing along with songs that have useful chunks of language?
5. Do you ever record yourself reading aloud and then listen critically to the results?
6. Is background music a way of concentrating your thoughts?
7. Have you ever made up your own music to help you memorise language?
8. Have you set new words to familiar tunes?

9. Can you recall language items by humming an associated tune, even under your breath in an examination room?

   (This trick can work for beginners memorising a series of words such as days of the week and grammatical patterns, and for more advanced learners wanting to memorise a piece of text that seems worthwhile.)

10. Do you like to tape lectures?

    (Many institutions have a policy against this because it can inhibit other students in tutorials.)

Tactile learners

Tactile learning has to do with our sense of touch.

1. Is it difficult for you to study unless you are physically comfortable?
2. Do you need to stand up and stretch quite often instead of sitting hunched up over the computer or your books for hours at a time.
3. Do you enjoy making the shapes of scripts in other languages such as Korean, Thai, Chinese and Japanese?

Kinesthetic learners

Some of the tactile learners' preferences are true too for kinesthetic learners.

1. Are movement and touching things important to you?
2. Can you study lying on your bed without falling asleep?
3. Do you enjoy working in different comfortable places each day?

Summary

Beware of putting yourself too closely into one category of learner or another. People are not agreed on how definite or how permanent these classifications are. In fact those who say that students should not slot themselves neatly into one category or another put forward the following reasons:

1. It is very difficult to reach agreement on where one style starts and another stops.
2. In different situations individuals use different styles. How did

you learn to use a computer, to ride a bicycle, to cook? It may be that in one context you liked taking risks while in another you wanted to know all the rules before starting, as we shall see later in the chapter.

3. Individual's styles of learning seem to change over time.
4. Reasons like the students' opportunities to learn and the educational systems they are part of could be the real reasons for what seem to be their preferred styles.

If you are one of the people who think that putting people into categories is too restrictive, then dip into all types and see which strategies help you to learn better. There are elements in all these descriptions that could be used by anyone.

One question to keep in mind as you read the following descriptions of learning styles is this: Do the descriptions suggest new ways of experimenting with language learning? The descriptions overlap, so it is not a question of finding one perfect description of your style.

Another consideration is choosing the people you study with outside class. If you see yourself as enjoying learning in a particular way, then when you are choosing friends to study with you have two choices. One is to study with those who enjoy learning your way. The other is to have a mixed group so that each person adds something different to the study group.

3.3 Making a difference: Successful strategies

The good news is that students themselves can make a difference. Before reading on to see what others, including successful language learners, have said, try answering these questions. Then as you read you can compare other people's experiences with your own.

1. What difference do you think learners can make to their own progress?
2. What can go wrong when you plan ways of studying?
3. Can you think of any ways of being an independent language learner even when you are learning in a class?
4. If you were given a questionnaire and asked about your learning strategies, what strategies would you report?

Student helplessness

At the early stages of language learning, the ideas you want to express will outstrip your ability to say things in a way that matches your chronological age. This is a feeling all language learners experience when they try to use the language. One student says, 'I felt I was in kindergarten.'

The phrase 'learner helplessness' has been used to describe a state of mind where students believe that all language learning is up to the teacher or the course book. This helplessness can take different forms. Here are some examples.

Student 1 believes he is no good at languages. His family has persuaded him that it is a good thing to have languages in his degree ('You'll be more employable') but he himself believes it's a hopeless situation. 'I just don't have the brains for languages,' he says whenever the test results come out.

Student 2's problem is more organisational. She says she doesn't know how to learn. She sees people no more intelligent than she is, doing better and she says, 'Ah! But they know how to study, I don't,' as if it was something you did or did not have for ever.

Student 3 probably thinks the language teacher is the one who should set all the tasks. He does what he is told and no more. If a class is cancelled he thinks that's an hour lost from learning time. It would never occur to him to take the initiative and go to do further study in the library.

The following suggestions are intended for all these types of helplessness.

Language learning used to consist of choosing a course you could have confidence in and waiting to see what methods the teacher introduced for you to learn by. However, as we have seen, teachers' and lecturers' methods are only part of the difference between successful and less successful language learning.

While an ability in languages, knowing some useful, and useless, tactics from previous experience in language learning, and good teaching methods all make a difference, researchers have found out quite a bit about the learner's own part in the process. To find answers to the question of why successful learners do so well, these researchers observe language learners both in and outside class, they ask the learners questions and they look at samples of their work. The answers they find are very encouraging. Language learners do have some control over their learning. The more we know about language learning, the more we realise that the learner has a very active part to play in the process even while sitting week by week in a course taught by someone else. Terms like 'learner autonomy' or 'learner independence' and 'self-access', which teachers are now using, summarise some of the changes in learners' roles. Let's see how you can practise some autonomy in your language learning.

Being independent as a learner

Think about what the word autonomy means. It suggests the idea of independence, of taking some responsibility for your own learning. This is different from independent courses of study where you send away for tapes and a set of exercises that you correct yourself. In fact those courses don't give much independence because you have to follow closely a course of study worked out by others and wait for them to return your marked work either by post or by e-mail. Autonomy goes further. It means that learners have some say in the way they learn, both inside and outside class. As one student expresses it,

> Take an active part in the learning process; teachers can only do so much.

Making use of any self-access arrangements in your department is part of being autonomous. Many language departments provide multimedia and other laboratories for students to use in their own time. By spending as much time as you want in the laboratory and by manipulating the learning materials to suit your own speed and style of learning, you have greater autonomy than if all your learning takes place in one classroom at fixed times. In the more sophisticated computer-assisted language-learning programmes you can choose how often to repeat information and you can practise answering. You can take the part of one person in a dialogue and then the other. You can select bits of information that you want to know more about and have it highlighted on the screen. One student's advice, to have as much exposure to the language as possible, sums up one of the purposes of unstructured laboratory time.

Let us see specifically some of the ways that students say they have been able to help themselves, starting with ways of thinking about the learning process, then moving on to organisational points, and finally social strategies. All of these ideas have something in common. Good learning habits are

planned rather than just happening,
systematic rather than random,
available to all students.

3.4 STRATEGIES FOR BETTER THINKING

Think about details

One important strategy used by successful language learners is that they notice and think carefully about the details of what they hear and read. They are the people who ask questions. Why did she say it that way instead of this way? What was the effect of that intonation on the listeners? What is the difference between the way the word is used here and the way it was used last time I met it? Having noticed these details, they are ready to start using the language in more subtle ways, incorporating the new points.

Link new learning with old

You may think that each time you turn the page in your textbook everything is new, but in fact everything builds on what you have learned already. When you learn a new sentence pattern, for example, think of what this is similar to, both in your own language and in the one you are learning. If you are a student of more than one foreign language you will be able to make connections across three languages. One example of making connections is the fascinating history of how days of the week got their names in different languages.

An idea: Try to make some connections. Is the source of the names you are learning in any way similar to the source in English?

Another link is between familiar words and the new words that they seem to be used with most often. For example, when you hear the word *old* in English, what do you expect the next word to be: *house, woman, clothes*? What are the most common associations of the word *old* in the new language you are learning. These links are part of learning the culture of the new language (see Chapter 14.)

Grade your tasks for difficulty

When you are reading and revising it is best to move from the easy to the more difficult. Try to predict the difficulty of a task. For example, any of the following features make a difference to how difficult you will find a reading passage:

> your previous knowledge of the subject,
> the length of the passage,
> the number of illustrations,
> support provided (summary, glossary . . .),
> the way you approach it (with or without a dictionary).

3.5 ORGANISATIONAL STRATEGIES

Getting to class

As one student put it, '*Go to lectures. Missing a few won't hurt but you'll regret it if you miss too many.*' People have all sorts of good reasons for not attending classes. See if your favourites are in this list.

There's a big assignment coming up
It is easy to skip lectures when the pressure is on to complete assignments and when the lecturer doesn't call the roll. Keep in mind that the main purpose of attending class is not to give pleasure to the lecturer, who, after all, will not be sitting the examination and who is already fluent in the language. The purpose is to improve your own language competence. The more exposure you get to the language, the better your skills will be. It may also be that today's lecture is very important for the next assignment, the one you'll be starting just as soon as this one is handed in.

The teacher never calls the roll
As soon as you read this student's excuse you will see the fallacy. Again, it's students who sit examinations, not teachers.

The class discussion is not stimulating
This can happen when slow students spend most of the time asking questions along the lines of 'What does this mean?' and 'Please explain this once again to me.' The answer to this problem is not to walk away

from the class but to pla
well as for others. Star
questions. Put a contrar
help of even one othe
discussion and involvem

The teacher never asks
It is true that in some tu
share of comments whil
a turn, try some of thes

   Learn and practise
      language. ('Just a
   Link your remarks t
   Ask the last speaker
      that mean . . . ?')

These are important conversational skills in any language. In genuine out-of-class conversations, being named to speak is only one way of getting a turn. If all you do is wait for the teacher to call your name in class, you won't have a chance to practise the phrases that you will need when you meet native speakers, especially those who just keep talking at their normal pace.

In summary, there are many reasons for attending class, including the fact that languages are not a subject where you can easily borrow someone else's notes to catch up with a missed session.

Time management

Good language learners know how to manage their time. They don't necessarily work longer hours than anyone else but when they intend to work that's what they do. They also plan for time off and for alternating periods of intense study with more relaxing periods in between. Here are examples of tasks you can alternate, depending on which you find more or less stressful.

   Talking in the new language with others,
   Listening to authentic texts and trying to get the main meaning,
   Learning new vocabulary,

Writing essays,
Writing translations,
Reading your set book,
Designing new resources for learning (see later in this chapter).

Accessing computer resources

As we have mentioned, most language departments have computer laboratory facilities. Depending on how sophisticated they are, here are some of the ways you can use them to learn new language, to practise in your head what you already know, and to monitor your progress. How many of the following are available to you?

Automatic speech recognition

Some software recognises your voice and then makes comments on it – a wonderful way of having feedback on your pronunciation. (If you can't do this on your computer, then you can still use the traditional way of recording your own voice on audiotape and listening to it.)

Word games

There are programs that allow you to learn new words and phrases by calling up topics of interest to you. Others give you a chance to check how much you know. For example, one program puts up the title of a piece of text and invites you to start filling in the screen by predicting the words that might appear. When you guess correctly, the words appear in the right place. Using an English-language example, if you saw the heading from a newspaper article 'Coup fears in . . .', you could ask yourself the following questions as a way of predicting what words might appear in the article.

What country might this be? (place names)
What actions are associated with coups? (verbs)
Who might be involved in a coup? (descriptions of people)
What emotions could be mentioned?

If you guess correctly even half a dozen words, then the screen starts filling up, which of course helps you to guess the next six. Some students learn quickly that typing in the small, predictable words like the articles (if your language has them) helps to provide a framework for intelligent prediction of what's left. This is just one example of a word game.

Interactive comic strips

Some computer programs allow you to hold virtual conversations with characters in comic strips. This is a comfortable stepping stone for students who feel shy about speaking up in a new language in front of others.

The Internet

Another rapidly-developing source of information for language learners is the Internet. This is a world-wide network of computers which anyone with a modem and a phone line can link to. If you don't already have a modem, it is a piece of equipment which you can buy for your computer, to connect it to a phone line. If your computer is connected to a school or university network, then you can be linked to the Internet easily.

With the correct software, anyone who can access the Internet can produce a website, which is a document containing information on any topic the writer chooses. It can include pictures, sounds, video clips, etc. This document is then available for viewing by anyone else with an Internet connection. Around the world, websites have been set up in different languages. One student reported the following in a short search:

> I did a five-minute search through Yahoo and found six sites in Italian, heaps in French and eight in Spanish but with links and categories I didn't explore probably yielding a lot more for all three languages.

Find a site with a subject that interests you in the language you are studying and start searching for yourself. Because of the vast number of websites, various search engines have been set up. These are programs which index the information contained in websites. Two examples are Yahoo (http://www.yahoo.com) and Altavista (http://www.altavista. digital.com). Yahoo indexes the names of sites. So, for instance, a search under 'French' gives all the site names containing the word 'French', including French departments at universities and polytechnics, French language courses, sites containing French literature and so on. This search engine is useful for finding sites on general topics.

Altavista is useful when searching for information on specific topics such as Medieval French Literature. It is more in-depth, indexing all the documents on each site. Thus when an Altavista search is done, it returns the Internet location of every document which contains the search item. For example, a search for 'French' results in about 360,000 individual documents.

Many sites also contain a page of links which provide the Internet addresses of other sites you might be interested in. You can click on a site with the mouse and you are automatically taken to the other website. After finding one site of interest, for example by using a search engine, the viewer can then follow the links provided to other sites of potential interest. The process of going through pages on sites then jumping via links to other sites is known as surfing the Net.

Some of these sites contain up-to-date information in current language written for native speakers of the language. If this sounds too much like reading a textbook, remember that websites also contain graphics, sound clips and interactive material. Many websites have been developed specifically for language learners. For instance, Travlang (http://www.travlang.com) provides learning materials for over 55 languages, including sound files for pronunciation, and links to a number of online translating dictionaries. An example of a page containing links indexed by language is available on Douglas Brick's site (http://www.speakeasy.org/~brick/Hot/foreign.html).

The best way to explore what is available is to sit down at a computer with Internet access and follow your nose. A wealth of information is available, it's just a matter of finding it.

Film and other resources

Movies and videos

As well as attending international film festivals you can borrow foreign-language videos to watch in your own time. If there are subtitles then you can view the video with or without that support. One student did this by covering the subtitles with paper before re-watching particular sections. Movies are a great opportunity to:

recognise familiar words,
guess the meaning of colloquialisms from the context,
start learning the clues that come from body language and facial
    expression in different languages,
pick up cultural information.

TV news

Do you have access to television programmes in the language you are learning? Many university language departments now have the facility to receive direct broadcasts from all round the world via satellite. If you are at one of these places then make the most of it because learners report that watching programmes such as the news is a great and quite painless way to learn.

If you also have Teletext and can turn it on and off, then your learning possibilities are even better. Instead of having to reach for the dictionary each time you are unsure of a word you can use all the clues available: the background pictures, the surrounding words and, of course, yesterday's news, because many items are a continuation of an ongoing story.

As well as the language you learn directly from watching news broadcasts, you will also have topics of current interest to discuss in your next conversation with native speakers or other language learners. Even if you let yourself off duty and become more absorbed in the pictures, the sounds of the language are still going into your mind.

TV dramas

If you are not so interested in the news you could become involved in watching a soap opera. These often have predictable themes so that it is not such a struggle to follow the meaning. Half an hour a day hearing people speak more or less authentic language about everyday, personal events gives you access to a particular type of language. The context is approximately the same each day, and the characters don't change much, but the events of their lives move around between several places in each episode. In short, watching soaps has the advantage of providing a relaxing environment which can balance all the intense study you do in other ways.

In the middle of the soaps there will probably be advertisements. Resist the urge to go and make coffee during this break. Students say that singing along with the advertisements gives them chunks of idiomatic language that pop back into their minds at the right moment.

Newspapers and magazines

Newspapers could be available in the reading room of public libraries if you live in a large centre. Make time to go there and read the sections that interest you. There may even be news about your own country written in the new language.

Your language department probably subscribes to some magazines or journals. In addition to these there could be special-interest magazines that you would enjoy reading because the topic is something that interests you anyway. Every language has its specialised magazines about sports, cars, architecture, nature and so on. Where are you going to find these magazines? You can now do computer searches which would allow you to track down some of this material free.

On the Internet, Yahoo lists magazines in categories too (autos, gardening etc.) but if you prefer getting glossy magazines through the post each month, get a subscription. Either way, you will be picking up some specialised language as well as plenty of general terms.

Make your own resources

As well as all these resources already prepared by others, you can make up some of your own. There are many ways of making up resources that will be useful to you: word cards for learning vocabulary, mind maps for learning structures, photocopies of material that you adapt in some way with highlighters and scissors. Many of these are explained in detail later in the book. However, there are also ways of adapting the materials in your textbook to make them more useful to your style of learning. For example, with access to a photocopier here are some tricks to try.

1. Copy a shortish article and cut the paragraphs up separately. Put them all in an envelope for a day or so and then try to reassemble them in the right order. Although this is listed as an organisational strategy it actually calls for careful thinking. As you are working out the order, you have to use all sorts of clues, some of them language clues, such as looking for linking words and phrases, and other more subtle clues of meaning. Just one warning. Make sure that the angle you cut the page at doesn't give you an additional clue and turn the whole exercise into a simple jigsaw assembly.

2. Photocopy the vocabulary lists at the end of each chapter in your textbook and fold them in two. Test yourself going from the other language to your first language and then vice versa.

3. Make up a three-column version of your vocabulary list, the third column being a phrase or sentence that uses the new word. Fold it

over so that you can check both your understanding and your ability to recall the word at the right time.

[**NB**: Remember that you may copy only isolated pages for your individual use.]

Making the most of human resources

Finally we look at all the sociable ways you can improve your learning through joining in activities and seeking out people.

Extra-curricular activities

Many students say that taking part in university plays in the foreign language was a wonderful way of practising. Find out, too, about class parties, speech contests, target-language-only lunches, and foreign film festivals.

Conversation groups

Some students still believe that it will spoil their language development to listen to other students' mistakes. That belief is outdated. The idea that native speakers are the only ones worth speaking with is based on an old-fashioned idea that the language part of our brain is like a clean slate and that anything non-perfect going onto it would contaminate the slate. We no longer believe that languages are learned in this way.

What are the benefits of using the new language with other students? You have a chance to:

hear different ideas and information,
clarify your own ideas by hearing other people's reactions to them,
work out meaning from many different ways of speaking,
take your listeners into account while speaking,
compare your own expressions with theirs,
express things more clearly if people don't understand you,
receive feedback on your language,
talk at a language level similar to your own.

A final reason for talking with other students has to do with cost. It is cheaper than hiring a special tutor or making *international telephone calls (expensive!)'* to contacts in another country as one student advises. If your money is restricted you could choose the cheaper advice to *'Speak as much as possible with native or competent speakers'* who include your fellow students. You could also imitate one student who got his girlfriend hooked on the language and culture, so that she became a language student and they could speak the new language together.

Finding native speakers

Are any of these people available to you?

Tourists who need guides speaking their language.
Spouses who have come to live in your country and want to use their own language sometimes.
Exchange students at local secondary schools from Germany, South America, and so on.
International students in other departments who would agree to language practice in return for help with their English.

Another source of native speakers is chat sites on the Internet.

4

LANGUAGE LEARNING:
MEMORY AND MOTIVATION

> *Why do some students seem very gifted in oral classes but score poorly on tests?*
> *Why does the person who was a weak student in high school language classes*
> *suddenly shine at university? Is it different methods of teaching? Is it a late*
> *development of talent? Often the difference between a successful and unsuccessful*
> *language learner has to do with memory and motivation. The discussion of*
> *language learning processes continues with these two topics.*

4.1 INFORMATION ABOUT MEMORY

Everyone has an anecdote about effective ways of remembering a
new language. Someone will mention an uncle who was fluent in
Russian because he played himself tapes of spoken Russian as he fell
asleep each night. Another person says the only way to learn is to go and
live in the country. In this first half of the chapter we'll consider
what part memory plays in learning a new language. The emphasis will
be on the sort of remembering that includes understanding, rather
than on rote learning, although people's impressive ability to recite
lists of irregular verbs has a place too. Learning is a more or less
permanent change which affects your responses as you speak. Memory
for language goes far beyond something which is stored in your
head. There are different types of memory. We'll compare two of these,
short-term and long-term memory, and show their relevance for
language learning.

Short- and long-term memory

We store ideas in our mind on a short-term or long-term basis. You can experience the difference between the two by giving yourself a test like this. Try to memorise the following list:

LFOGTADONYKMOCEW

Then cover the page and *immediately* try to recall those letters. You will probably find that the ones you recall best are the letters at the beginning and the end of the list. We call this the serial position effect. It has been said that most of us can remember only seven items encoded in this way because that is the limit of short-term memory. If you arrange the same letters into small groups that have something in common, like this:

CAT DOG MONKEY WOLF

you will find the list much easier to remember. Try the same thing a bit later in the day and the words you can still recall are those that have moved into your long-term memory. Those you could not remember immediately won't be amongst those you will remember later. It is likely that you will remember the first items but the last on the list were probably in short-term memory and therefore lost.

The point of this experiment is just to demonstrate the difference between remembering items for a short or a long time. It is not meant to suggest that memorising lists of isolated words is a great idea. When will you ever want to recite a list of words in order, much less backwards? You store words in your memory so they can be used in everyday language.

Your memory stores some information that you are not interested in remembering. For example, it doesn't help your language learning to recall that today's lesson started on page 36 but you may have remembered the number just the same. Remembering the date of your next assignment might be more useful.

Your aim in language learning is to move things into your long-term memory ready for use. One thing that moves the information from short- to long-term memory is repetition. In the language class the repetition of new items takes many forms. You may be reading aloud with the teacher or listening to someone else read. You will probably be writing down important points and even recopying them later in ways that help you to remember. Then there is saying something several times. In a language, this sort of repetition is likely to lead to better memory if you are thinking of the meaning at the same time. The exceptions to this are the lists that are part of the early stages of language learning, such as numbers and months of the year. Even these will be moving quickly into frequent use in more meaningful ways than lists.

There are three aspects of language learning that need to be encoded in long-term memory. These are your verbal, motor and social skills. Most people think about remembering and using new words (verbal skills), and the social part, using language for communication, but in some language learning it is important to remember new motor skills. For example, if you have written only in the Roman script up to now, your memory has to be developed to write new symbols legibly and reasonably fast. Motor skills are involved in pronouncing new sounds.

Recalling and forgetting

What really counts in learning a language is whether you can remember something when required, which usually means that the information encoded in the mind has to be retrieved at two main points – (1) in the context of tests when provided with various prompts, and (2) in the context of the sort of situations we face every day in our own language – joining in group conversations, writing letters, talking on the phone.

Sadly, forgetting is a part of the process of storing and trying to retrieve items from your memory. The good news is that forgetting trails away. Plenty is forgotten immediately after it has been 'filed' but repetition (returning to the items) can replace them in your memory. Also, if you try to recall things at spaced intervals they have more chance of staying there, because memory is affected by the amount and spacing of time spent on learning as well as by the depth of processing.

You have to return to new language many, many times, processing it in different ways to avoid boredom, in order to remember it for long enough to use it. The details of how long is an optimum length to leave between each practice are not precise but the general message is this. Space out your revision time. This makes the idea of breaks from study sensible as well as pleasant. Running round the block with the dog or making a social telephone call to a friend are only two types of legitimate interruption you can dream up for yourself. Reinforcement of learning comes when you return to your study a second, third and fourth time.

All this memory work will stand you in good stead when you are using language for speaking and writing and of course, the big one, for examinations. Language examinations rarely call for information that has been committed to rote memory. You will be tested instead on your ability to demonstrate understanding of everything that is written or said in the language.

Language learners are usually more interested in learning for meaning than in rote learning, which is associated with groups of learners reciting lists from which they cannot retrieve a single item later when they are listening, speaking, reading or writing. Whatever methods students use to remember new language, it's the retrieval that is visible to others that counts, so we turn now to consider what makes it possible to retrieve new learning and what makes it difficult.

Essentially, remembering depends on finding effective ways of storing the new learning. The better the items have been encoded, the easier it is to retrieve them. This is not a parallel with a bedroom where everything is lying haphazardly in any place but the owner can easily locate a shirt that needs ironing or a dictionary lying underneath something else. Although we may think that some people have haphazard minds that lead them to express random thoughts throughout the day, the results of language tests suggest a strong link between logical and in-depth storage and quick retrieval.

As part of thinking about ways of remembering we can also review what is known about forgetting, on the principle that knowing what can go wrong is part of knowing how to avoid it. One problem is with associating things that shouldn't be associated. This can happen when students start to learn a foreign language that is very close to their own. Particular words that resemble each other in form but not meaning are sometimes called 'false friends'. Between English and French, Italian and Spanish, German and Dutch there are many examples of false pairs. It is worth highlighting these when you are learning. Some language dictionaries or textbooks may even supply lists of them. Certainly the teacher will usually draw attention to them as they appear.

The other reasons for forgetting could be summarised as the opposite of the factors listed at the start of this section. People forget things because they have not learned helpful ways of remembering, because they believe that any effort put into memory work is artificial in the context of language learning or because they do not like the subject or at least the parts of the subject that need memorising.

4.2 FACTORS AFFECTING MEMORY

The way people use their memory depends on a number of factors: their cultural preferences (what emphasis was given to rote learning in your early teaching and schooling), their attitudes to memorising (positive and negative) and to what they are trying to remember, the time spent on trying to remember, and finally the meaningfulness of what is being learned.

Cultural and personal preferences

Through most of this book the assumption seems to be made, that English is your first language. This may not be the case. Many people are studying a third or fourth language, having already mastered English as a foreign language, and this book is written for them too. A number of students in our survey spoke languages other than English from childhood. Like them, you may come from a tradition where memorising passages of language has been a part of your education from a young age. You may be accustomed to learning lengthy passages off by heart and possibly even reciting them to an audience. Actors develop the same skill. In that case, make the most of it. All you have to decide is what is worth memorising.

In addition to cultural traditions, people's individual attitudes to memory are also shaped by personal beliefs. For example, some people think that memorising is the opposite of understanding and shy away from it in the context of language learning. They say, 'Don't memorise it. Try to understand it,' as if the two were mutually exclusive. This attitude is sometimes based on childhood memorising of poetry or mathematical formulae or grammar rules which didn't seem to mean much. In one high-school French class students had to take it in turns to call out rules of pronunciation such as '-eu- sounds œ in French'. As we shall see, it *is* possible to recite something off and actually understand what you are saying.

Attitude

Another factor affecting attitude towards memorising is what people expect of their own ability. People say, 'I can't learn the vocabulary lists. I've always had a bad memory.' Perhaps what they mean is that they have not learned ways of harnessing their memories. Let's consider some of the ways in which attitude can make a new language easier or more difficult to remember. These range from your attitude towards the language and its speakers, to your attitude towards a particular lesson. Let us assume that you really want to learn a language. However critical you may feel of the methods being imposed on you, you can help overcome short-term annoyance by keeping your eye on the long-term goal and your positive feelings about the language.

At a more specific level, memorising a set of words will be easier if you have some strong reason for needing those words. Students who report using their new language in the country where it is spoken (as in Chapter 1) say that needing the words for their work is an important motivator for remembering. For you, in the short-term it could be that next week's test acts as a goad.

One successful student of Japanese had this to say about the connection between memory and motivation.

To be honest, in my learning of Japanese I had to use a lot of memorization, especially for learning the written characters. I found that the overwhelming predictor of success (apart from requiring a certain level of aptitude, which a large proportion of people have I believe) was motivation.

Time

The student quoted above is making the point that increased motivation leads to more time spent on the memory aspects of the language. If the time was also spent in ways that really do help memory, then the results are pleasing. The time spent trying to remember is an obvious factor in whether or not things stick, but time cannot be measured just in its total amount. As you will know from studying long hours and late at night before a test, there comes a time when spending longer is no good. Spacing out the learning and applying it between bouts of concentrated study are also important. Many tests are done by educational psychologists to see whether there is an optimal time for studying before taking a break but, as experience has probably taught you, there is no quick answer. Some people can concentrate for longer than others, some days are hotter than others, some information is harder to remember and so on.

Apart from the actual hours spent there is also the question of repetition, which, as we have seen, is an important part of memorising.

Very little of a language is learned from a single meeting. There needs to be repetition in both the language received (through reading and listening) and the language used (speaking and writing).

Meaningfulness

Another factor to consider is meaningfulness. Whatever you are trying to memorise, give it meaning. If you have twenty words you must know by tomorrow, make up a sentence to include as many of them as possible. If today's grammar rule is difficult, try to find a short sentence or two to memorise, particularly if you can include two structures that you are likely to confuse.

Amount and quality

Of course trying to remember long chunks of language is usually considered harder than learning short passages or lists but even this advice needs to be qualified. Long passages where the meaning is important can be easier to learn than a list of unconnected words. A list of words can be easier or more difficult depending on how it is put together. Words that can easily be confused take longer to learn in the same list, for example.

Depth of processing

Depth of learning in language learning means paying attention to meaning. Say you are studying with a friend and you decide to check each other on yesterday's learning. An example of a superficial question would be, 'What was the word starting with T that was used to describe so-and-so?' A deeper type of question would be, 'Give me a sentence of your own to sum up yesterday's reading passage.' As we shall see in the chapter on vocabulary learning, depth of processing is also increased if you try to work out word meanings for yourself before checking with the dictionary.

4.3 TECHNIQUES FOR REMEMBERING

The general message about techniques for remembering is 'the more, the better'. There are dozens of mechanisms by which people help themselves to remember. These include mnemonics created by turning the letters of a list or sentence into a word that is easy to recall, and making up a poem (of sorts) to remind yourself of which German prepositions are followed by the dative case and which by the accusative. This is an area of memory where being an original thinker is a great help. One Roman general, so the story goes, could address every one of his 35,000 soldiers by name thanks to mnemonics.

In this section we'll look at some techniques for remembering. In particular we'll see that the way items are stored affects your chances of recalling them. We'll look at different ways of organising and visualising information. In the chapter on vocabulary there are further details about memory and learning new words.

Look for patterns

Good storage depends partly on finding patterns. There are patterns in the grammar of a language, in its sound system and in the way its words are put together. In an ideographic language these patterns are visual and in phonetic languages there are sound patterns that are repeated from one word to the next either as a sign of meaning or as a sign of the word's role in a sentence. Children see patterns in their own language long before they think consciously about form. If English is your first language you probably moved through saying 'he taked it from me', to 'he tooked it from me', and then 'he took it from me', as you saw the pattern of the sound at the end of words. At other times, when the pattern is not so obvious, you can make one up for yourself.

Make associations

One popular method that language learners use involves making associations. They trigger the associative networks of the memory in various ways. Some of the associations may seem trivial, but if they work that's all that matters. People will recall that it was a hot afternoon when they read a particular poem and from there they remember some of the words they met for the first time in that poem.

This means even these trivial and seemingly irrelevant details can be useful. Some students, when they organise their lecture notes, jot down details of who the lecturer was and what room they were in, and these background details turn out to be valuable later as a way of recalling the language of the lesson. Many people report that even some sort of non-meaning association helps them. In language this can include thinking that the new word reminds you of something quite different and then picturing that different thing as a memory trigger. Thus someone who keeps forgetting that the Italian past participle for the verb to do is 'fatto' could start picturing an overweight person who has just completed a task.

Use visual imagery

That brings us to the use of your visual memory, which was mentioned earlier in relation to learning styles. Flashcards with pictures or symbols on them are a good memory jog for visualising. As soon as you see a particular picture you remember the word that goes with it, or better still, the sentence.

Many students use flashcards for individual words, but not so many report using them for recalling whole sentences. The more unusual the sentences you make up to remember new words, the more strikingly you will be able to picture the action. If you enjoy exercising your memory, try reading aloud a whole paragraph as you stare at a picture. If you work your way up through small to longer paragraphs you could be surprised at the results. Again, make sure that the language is going to be either interesting or useful to you in future, to make the job worthwhile.

Use all the senses

Associating what you try to remember with particular sounds, sights, smells, taste and touch is another technique that students report. As we mentioned earlier, activating the senses as a means of remembering is recommended in language learning.

Much of what is written about sensory memory refers mainly to words and grammar. A more subtle aspect of memory is pronunciation. Learners may find they can make the sounds very well under controlled conditions but fail to make them clearly in a chain of spontaneous speech. This is particularly true in the early stages of language learning and with sounds that are quite different from those in your own language. Remembering the sounds of a tonal language is a good example. The teacher gives you feedback praising the way you have distinguished the rising and falling tone. 'Ah!' you think, with a flashback to Eliza Dolittle in *Pygmalion*, who had trouble with the vowels of English, 'At last I've got it.' Then the next time you meet a native speaker that person has to keep asking you to repeat yourself and you know you have not yet mastered the tone. There is more on the topic of pronunciation in Chapter 9.

Apply information

A further memory prod is to apply what you are learning immediately to a particular aspect of language use. In other words, ask yourself when you are most likely to need this expression. Many students recommend:

applying rules to sentences,
making up examples,
using a format to write sentences.

The easiest application is by topic. Particular sets of words and phrases will be useful for talking or writing about political themes, about human relationships or about something as practical as meals. These will not all come from the same lesson, but you can keep returning to a theme, making up more and more varied sentences.

Another application is to classify new language according to the purpose it will be most useful for, such as asking questions or expressing complaints. This is one way of thinking about particular structures of the language. To use English as an example, the conditional is useful for expressing wishes ('I would rather . . .'. 'What would you suggest?') and the past tense is more common for narrating events from yesterday ('We saw the bus but it didn't stop.'). This is an oversimplification of grammar rules, of course, because as we know, many people recount narratives using the English present tense ('I'm dashing along and all of a sudden who comes past but . . .').

Link new learning with old

Finally, there is the notion of making up frameworks for collecting new words. It could work like this with a chapter in your textbook headed 'Industrial Waste'. Before starting to read, recall all that you already know on the topic from other general knowledge or other subjects you have studied. Your thinking could range from the international to the personal:

> I remember they talked about industrial waste at a world summit meeting last year.

> Haven't some rivers in the world been cleaned up in the second part of this century?

> Near where I live there's a factory chimney that gives off unpleasant fumes.

Try to recall specifically some of the words you have learned in the new language that could appear in such an article. For example, you might recall for any of these:

> smoke, fumes, pollute, discharge, clear up, factories, oil, poisonous.

Whether you write these words on paper or just say them to yourself as a quick free recall, the process can give your mental framework the chance to organise the new information you are about to read or hear. We call this 'making use of your associative networks'.

Another way of thinking of a framework is to call it a matching exercise, not in the simple type of task where you find a word that means the same as another one but rather in terms of finding words that go together. They might go together because they come from the same word, or because one is often followed by the other, as in 'steep path', 'steep hill', 'a steep rise' and so on.

Another example of making associations is if the language you are learning uses different forms of greeting for different people according to how well you know them or how old they are. You could associate a new phrase for saying farewell to strangers with one you already know for saying farewell to close friends. The chapter on reading, later in the book, expands this idea of making associations.

4.4 MOTIVATION AND ATTITUDE

We move on now to thinking about motivation. Essentially, lack of motivation drags people down in their language learning and high motivation pulls them up. The good news is that, like memory, motivation is not something you either have or don't have.

Motivation is a topic you will know plenty about from experience, even if you haven't studied psychology. We talk about being motivated or unmotivated for all the tasks of life from making our bed to applying for a job. Motivation includes not just deciding to learn a language, but all the endless tasks associated with keeping trying. Motivation in language learning is slightly different from motivation in other subjects. Just reading more foreign-language textbooks or writing longer essays is only part of the story. Success in language learning means being able to communicate in a natural context, whether the context is writing letters, or exchanging conversations, or communicating with people all over the world through e-mail.

Different kinds of motivation and orientation

If you have studied psychology you will know about different kinds of motivation. Let's see how understanding more about motivation can improve your language learning. Motivation starts with your original reason for choosing to study this language. Let's assume that since you have signed on for a language course, you would like to pass. Before reading about different types of motivation, reflect on your reasons for studying a language and check back to Chapter 1 to see other people's reasons.

Some of the motives given by students may seem more powerful than others but any reason that is important to you can work. The students who said 'I couldn't think of anything else to study,' and 'My parents wanted me to study it,' will have to work harder at finding their own motivation. Studies done in different countries suggest that motivation can take many forms. The following summaries and examples don't do justice to the topic of motivation in general but they do highlight factors that could be important for students. They help you answer the question, 'Why am I learning this language?'

Achievement motivation

Students A and B are both studying languages because they are good at them. Their school studies showed that they did better in languages than in some other subjects in the curriculum. Which of these students sounds like you?

1. Student A loves to succeed. Because she likes to have top grades in all her tests she works very hard at all her assignments and prepares

for oral examinations by listening to tapes and setting aside time immediately before the exams to use the language with others. Usually that works.

2. Student B also loves to succeed but unfortunately this drive is so strong that she cannot bear any kind of failure. For her, failure means an A grade instead of an A +. The result is that when she comes to an oral examination she is nervous and comes across as not being a fluent communicator.

Both students are motivated to achieve, but in one case the motivation is a help while in the other it is a hindrance. If you are like Student B it is up to you to find a balance between your wish to do well and the anxiety that stops you from making the most of your ability.

Integrative orientation

Whether you are learning the language for what is called integrative purposes, which means you want to identify with other people who belong to that culture, or for instrumental purposes, where learning the language is a means to an end such as getting a job, you have just as much chance of success. In our study some learners who were achieving high grades report one reason and some another. All of them were achieving B + or higher.

If you are studying a language because you want to identify with the people who speak the language and with their culture, then you are like some of the students in our study who gave reasons like this:

Speaking another language is discovering a new (personal and foreign) identity.

[That] culture interests me.

I love Italy, Italians, Italian culture, art history etc.

Their comments, and others' like them, show that appreciating the culture and people can be a strong motivating force.

A few students are already part of another culture through their family connections, but have missed out on learning the language.

I am half Spanish and unfortunately did not learn the language as a child.

I wanted to learn more about my cultural heritage.

Making connections with your ancestry can be a strong motivation for study. You can make the most of this sort of motivation by keeping in touch with relatives who still speak the language.

Instrumental orientation

Being instrumentally oriented means that you are learning a language because it will be useful to you in one or more ways. Students with an eye on future employment make comments like these:

The ability to speak Mandarin will be a useful tool in the future.

Useful to an international business degree.

[To be] a teacher.

It's an up-and-coming practical language [which] will be the second most widely spoken language by the year 2000.

If you are finding it hard to see where your language studies might lead you, then take time to visit the campus careers adviser to find out employment possibilities for graduates of your language.

Intrinsic and extrinsic motivation

Another way of looking at your reasons for learning a language is to see which of these statements applies better to you:

1. I am learning Chinese because I love learning languages. It doesn't matter which language I learn. I just enjoy the learning.

2. I am learning Chinese because it's a language that will take me where I want to go. It's a bit boring doing the study but it will be worthwhile in the end.

If you agree with the first speaker, then your motivation is intrinsic. If the second one is you, then extrinsic motivation is working for you. We can't say that one form of motivation is better than another but whatever your reason is, keep focusing on it so that you can overcome feelings of boredom or frustration on the way.

Your own motivation

Perhaps you are one of the many students who don't have just one reason. You may want to appreciate the people and the culture and may also think the language could be useful. Perhaps you are studying a language because you are good at learning languages or because you enjoy the actual process without worrying too much about what that language might be. Your reasons may be different for each language you are studying. One student gives these reasons for learning two different languages:

Japanese: Interesting culture / easy to learn.

Spanish: Good sound, widely spoken

Even students who have unusual reasons for language study can do well. The following remarks were made by people who were getting good marks.

I liked the sound of the language.

Had learned and enjoyed [these languages] before. Couldn't think of anything else to study.

A friend dared me to take the course with him. So I did.

It's easy to learn.

To pick up marks.

Choosing the language to study, with all the reasons we have considered, is only part of being motivated. People could feel very excited about a certain culture, its people and its language but it stands to reason that without some effort there will be no results.

How do feelings affect language progress? Is this integrated?

Everyone reacts differently to the learning situation, ranging from anxiety to a relaxed frame of mind. Not all of these differences are fixed, of course. Some people can temporarily be in a highly anxious state about their language learning because of circumstances in their lives that have nothing to do with the classroom, while others tend to be in a more permanently anxious state about life.

Although some students don't worry about what they will do with the language later, for many, part of being interested involves feelings of the relevance of their chosen language for their future. Relevance also includes affiliation with other people. The learner might say, 'Am I really getting closer to communicating with other people through my language learning?'

Your feelings are also affected by whether you feel you are making progress and, if not, whose fault it is. Teachers often have a struggle between short-term and long-term relevance for students in foreign-language classes. The actual out-of-class application of what is learned comes later, although this has become easier through the use of technology to bring news programmes by satellite from all over the world in many languages. Starting your course with an expectancy of success is certainly more promising than believing from the start that you will be a failure.

Identify and attack your setbacks

Students starting out to learn a new language range from the very confident ('I was good at physics. Why shouldn't I be good at languages?') to the pessimistic ('Everyone says only clever people can learn languages.'). Everyone, those who start confidently and those who start diffidently, will have setbacks. It's a case of being ready for them.

What can go wrong?

Why is it that some people who seem to have less ability than others actually have better results? What can people do if they feel unmotivated? What about those who are so motivated that fear of failure stops them from doing their best? You need general motivation to spend time on your language learning, in particular to learn vocabulary and master the sentence patterns of the language. You also need motivation when things go wrong, just as you did when you toppled off your bicycle as a child. Knowing ahead of time what the problems are is a help. Remember the old saying 'To be forewarned is to be forearmed.' Start by picturing all the small frustrations you will face and reminding yourself of how you can view them positively. There can be many setbacks in language learning, and not being understood the first time you speak to someone is one of them. Start to picture all the things that go wrong for language learners from time to time, so that you are ready to motivate yourself past them.

You have to ask someone to repeat three times.
Someone asks you to repeat three times.
You have a low test mark after studying all night.
Some phrases you knew a month ago have escaped from your
    memory.

Many of these mini-defeats have clear explanations that you can easily deal with. Asking people to repeat is part of communication even in our first language. Not getting enough sleep before a test is a sure way of failing to do justice to what you know. Remembering new information depends on using it from time to time. After a month without being used It's not surprising that the phrases have disappeared.

Let's return to the comparison with learning to ride a bicycle. Think back to the times when your learning didn't go so well. If you learned before trainer wheels were invented, you probably had some falls. When you fell off and grazed your knee you had several choices. You could throw the bicycle to the back of the shed and announce that you would never ride it again. You could go inside for a while to patch up your injured knee before coming out for another go. A third option was to pick yourself up immediately and try again. What does this have to do with language learning?

First you need to know what aspects of language learning are like falling off a bicycle. Here are some disappointments that learners report.

I tried to talk with a visiting German student but she didn't understand me.

After staying up till midnight learning for a test I got a bare 50%.

I still can't make out the difference between two particular tones of Chinese.

If you are ready for these setbacks, if you know that, like riding a bicycle, language learning is a skill that develops gradually through making mistakes, then you won't be surprised when they come. Let's look first at the three students whose setbacks are listed above. What do they need to know?

Nobody understands me

Here is an imaginary student (*D* for defeatist) talking to another imaginary student (*R* for realist).

D: I met a German student in the cafeteria the other day and tried to talk to her. She couldn't understand a word I said.

R: What did you do?

D: I just walked away. No point in staying.

R: Do you normally walk away when people don't understand you in English?

D: No. I usually try again.

R: You should try that next time you meet a German student. What did you say to her anyway?

D: I was trying to tell her about my holiday in Germany but I'd only got as far as the airport bit when she asked me what I was saying.

R: So you understood her question? Well that's a start.

Notice that *D* focused on what was going wrong rather than what was going right. Also he overlooked the fact that we don't usually go up to strangers and start talking about our holidays without setting the scene first. In his eagerness to talk he had overlooked a basic aspect of communication with strangers that he probably knows in his own language. It could be summed up like this.

1. Find out what you have in common.
2. Say something you think may be of interest to the stranger.
3. Judge from the response whether they are interested.

Hard study gets me nowhere

Students often panic the night before a test and sit up too late studying. It may work for some people in some subjects but to perform in a language you need to be fresh. Do your best until the clock says it's a reasonable time for sleeping and then rely on all the work that has gone before.

I keep making the same mistakes

It's very unmotivating to be going over and over the most difficult aspects of a language and making no progress. Some things, like the differences between tones, need to be attacked in small bites. Ignore the difficulties for a while. In the case of two tones you can't distinguish, try listening to them in context for a while before isolating them again for special study.

Other setbacks are more general. Let's consider what they are and see how the self-blaming student and the student with a more positive attitude might deal with each.

I feel stupid speaking in another language

Self-consciousness is quite common with language learners. It can be felt by people who seem to be successful as well as people who see themselves as not doing well. It leads to the situation where the shy person won't speak even when chances arise. The more positive student, on the other hand, uses self-talk like this: 'I'm not so important that everyone is interested in the way I talk. What they want to hear is the content of my message.'

I hate to be less than perfect in tests and examinations

The phenomenon of wanting to be perfect all the time often strikes quite successful students. They have a deep-seated fear of failure. They are so motivated that whenever they think they may do less than perfectly in a test or assignment they become worried to the point of not doing their best.

This is a complicated situation. There's nothing wrong with aiming high as long as the occasional 51% grade doesn't set you back to the point where you can't concentrate on your studies. One low test mark is not the end of your language career. Try self-talk and talking to others. Remind yourself that what counts in the long term is not marks for a particular assignment but using language in real situations. In extreme cases, such as students whose fear of letting their family down almost paralyses them, it is sensible to talk to a counsellor.

If people don't understand me I know it's all my fault

When you are speaking in your own language and another person doesn't understand, you probably don't start by blaming yourself, but in a new language that is often what happens. Think of all the factors that make listening difficult: the surroundings are noisy, the listener's hearing may not be 100 per cent or, as in the case of the student trying to talk about his holiday, the listener doesn't know enough about the topic.

Provide your own motivation

If you are someone who needs to motivate yourself, here are some of the tactics that can work.

Study with a friend

Studying a language with a friend is more than just having company in the same room. Many aspects of language study work better with two or three people. For example:

Exchange original ways of remembering word meanings.
Test each other's vocabulary and phrases.
Speak the language for a set period of time with no English allowed.
Try to work out new word meanings from a reading passage before
    turning to the dictionary.

Reward yourself after each hour of concentrated study

Breaks are important in any kind of study. After each hour reward yourself in whatever way is most appealing. Here are some common 5-minute rewards:

a cup of coffee,
a quick phone call,
a short bike ride,
5 minutes of TV sport,
walking the dog,
some task with visible results such as lawnmowing.

Remove distractions

Only you know what your most frequent distractions are, but hunger is a common one. Listening to songs in the foreign language while you have a food break could make you feel still on target while stopping the distraction of hunger.

Play music in the background

Although the music you are listening to may have nothing to do with the target language, it can put you into a relaxed frame of mind. Some methods for language learning even have listening to music built in as part of the process. Here is one student's advice:

> To encourage myself to learn lists of vocabulary I listened to music at the same time, as this method is boring and does not require concentration.

Focus on aspects of the culture

Some of the ideas students report for keeping themselves motivated go beyond just the language. Here are two ideas.

> I try to cook Spanish food.

> To feed interest in the country I look at posters, pictures, articles, books.

Build on your basic motivation

Long term, it can also help to keep reminding yourself of your basic motivation for learning the language and make that work for you. For example, if your motivation is mainly intrinsic then challenges, curiosity and interest will work for you. Make yourself read beyond the course. Search out sources of material that are slightly beyond your present level so that your brain has to work harder to find the meaning. Some Internet sources could be useful. If you are sporty, look for a sports page and so on. Make your natural curiosity work for you.

Look for motivation in the wider world

Keep your interest alive by watching movies, and taking time to have contact with native speakers. In some universities and schools there are learning exchanges. You can provide conversation in English for overseas students, and in exchange they spend an hour another day talking their language with you. If you combine this with lunch then it doesn't even take extra time. The Internet provides further opportunities for conversational exchanges in a form of the language that is halfway between writing and speaking. If you have access to these facilities, make the most of them.

Acknowledge your weaknesses

If you like your work to be fairly easy, then choose a language which you don't think will be too challenging. If you find it hard to work for lengthy periods, make up a study programme that divides your learning into pleasant sized chunks.

Focus on your successes

As one student found, once you start to succeed, motivation will take care of itself because success is a great incentive.

Hard work was generally rewarded with higher grades.

You may also get motivated by finding that you really can communicate with or understand native speakers of the language. Several students report seeking out this kind of contact.

I had Japanese friends.

Shy students now find that communicating on the Internet is helpful in overcoming their fear of using the language.

What about circumstances beyond your control?

We have mentioned more than once a possible mismatch between the teacher's methods and yours. Do any of these complaints sound like yours?

We have to do pointless classroom activities.
The teacher will never correct us.
All our tutorials are at 8 a.m. I'm hardly awake then.
The classes are too big.
A few students do all the talking in tutorials.

It's hard to feel motivated if you feel that the learning activities you are being asked to do have no point to them. It may be that the activity really is helpful to language learning but you have not been told what the point is. For example, some people still believe that unless the teacher corrects every mistake they make in speech or in writing, then there is no point to the exercise, and yet there are many good reasons for not doing this. Many teachers separate the part of the lesson where they focus on accuracy from the part where fluency is more important.

Many of the laboratory facilities for language learning are organised so that students can decide for themselves how to work through the available materials. Multi-media laboratories with their tapes and computer programs mean that language learners can work interactively instead of just pressing a button and waiting for the program to run through. Here are a couple of ways of working in a multi-media laboratory.

Repeat a programme for different purposes

As you listen, or listen and watch for the second time, vary your role.

Repeat with the speakers.
Stop the tape and try to predict what they will say next.
Turn down the sound to pick up meaning from the context and body language.

Focus on particular language points

When you are reading or listening, decide to listen to the way a particular thing is done. For example, if the video lesson presents strangers meeting you could choose to focus on one of these:

intonation,
choice of topics,
turn-taking,
pauses between speakers.

Over to you

In summary, it would be easy to think that motivation is something you have or you haven't got in relation to language learning. However, as we have seen, there are many kinds of motivation and many ways of increasing your own. It's not realistic to imagine that everything about studying languages, or any other subject for that matter, will be pleasurable the whole time, but as one student says,

> Enjoying the language made lessons and difficulties worthwhile and enjoyable in the end.

5

SETTING GOALS AND MEASURING PROGRESS

Some students measure their success in language learning by the marks they gain in tests through the years. Others try self-assessing in various ways. They might keep a record of the number of words they have learned or notice that they are now reading at a higher level, or they might try themselves out in communication with native speakers and judge their success that way. This section talks about the close connection between setting learning goals and measuring progress. To put it more simply, if you don't know what your aim is you won't know whether you have reached it.

In the last chapter we talked about motivation, and how your reasons for learning a language can affect the way you learn and the progress you make. We now move more specifically to considering how you can set goals within your course and then see how well you are reaching them. Halfway between setting and measuring there is the question of how you will reach your goals. In this chapter we suggest practical ideas.

5.1 WHAT ARE YOUR GOALS?

The course you have joined will have its own goals. Sometimes these are made clear to students, sometimes not. Regardless of these course goals it will help you to think what your own are and how you might reach them.

From general to specific goals

General goals relate to your purposes for learning the language. We looked at some of these in Chapters 1 and 5. From these general reasons come more focused goals such as these:

By the end of this course I want to be able to use this language with native speakers for the following purposes:

for social relations,
to carry out business transactions,
to understand reasonably difficult spoken and written material.

You can then set yourself some even more specific goals with ways of measuring them. These let you know when you are making progress. For example, you could decide you want to:

read [decide what] . . . without a dictionary,
speak with an accent that people can understand,
conduct e-mail conversations with native speakers,
improve note-taking in Spanish lectures,
write essays that are more to the point,
take more part in the oral classes,
extend vocabulary for talking about literature.

Goals can also refer to areas of your language use that you want to improve. Writing them down can help pinpoint both weaknesses, strengths and the level you want to reach for each goal. For example, if you are someone who hesitates to speak much, then write something quite specific and measurable such as 'to speak at least three times in each tutorial next week'. On the other hand, if you are someone who enjoys talking you could set your goal in terms of choosing more occasions to talk outside class. In order to be measurable, your general goals need to be broken down into more specific goals. You know whether or not you have spoken three times in a tutorial.

Set some goals that go beyond the number of words learned or pages written. Think how you want to develop in terms of confidence, of cultural awareness, and, last but not least, how you want to improve as a language learner ready for the next language you choose to learn.

Wording your goals

If you are interested in measuring your goals, then you need to state to what degree and at what level you want to complete them. Therefore, instead of writing them in general terms, try asking yourself some specific questions like these.

> What do I want to know about the form of the language by the end of this semester?
> How many terms for talking about language would I like to learn?
> In what contexts do I want to use the language in the next few weeks?
> Which of my fears about speaking in conversations do I want to overcome by the end of the year?

The more specific you make these goals, the easier it will be later to see if you have reached them.

Linking goals with the course requirements

When you are studying a language as part of a course leading to a qualification, you need to know what is required to pass the course. For example, you could spend hours with a tape-recorder repeating sounds, when the oral examination rewards students for being able to hold a fluent conversation regardless of their pronunciation. Perhaps the occasional slip in pronunciation is not important. You need to know. What is required of you during the year? Does tutorial attendance and participation count for the final grade? How about assignments in the computer laboratory?

Similarly you need to know what is required in the written end-of-year examination. Go to previous examination papers (making sure that the format is going to be the same this year) and analyse the questions. Table 5.1 shows, as an example, analysis of one second-year university language examination. You can see quite clearly from this sort of check what they want and what the gap is between that and your present knowledge. The next step is to decide on the best preparation for each part of the examination. Some of the preparation goes on all through the year and some is at the last minute.

TABLE 5.1 ANALYSIS OF ONE LANGUAGE EXAMINATION

Task	Skills, Knowledge and Strategies
1. Translation	Idiomatic language Inferring meaning for unknown words Writing for total meaning
2. Read a passage / Answer questions	Vocabulary and structure Reading for overall meaning Reading for detail
3. Composition	Understanding the question Making a fairly quick choice Thinking of ideas Using known language to compensate for the new words and structures

Goals for learning opportunities

Part of the goal-setting can be planning opportunities to learn. For example, here is a list of things you could plan to do over a certain period of time in order to improve your language.

Read —— articles in a magazine.
Spend —— each week talking —— with other students.
Listen to foreign language broadcasts —— times a week.
Write without stopping for five minutes each day.

Notice that some of these relate to what you do and others to how long you do it for. You can set more difficult goals by making your tasks more challenging and by spending longer on them.

It is easy to think that all the planning of tasks to learn and practise language are done by the teacher. We look now at opportunities you can organise for yourself that go beyond the basic course requirements. These include tasks you can do by yourself, in pairs or in small groups of learners. The suggestions concentrate on tasks where meaning is important, not memorising symbols and practising difficult sounds, which is a part of the early stages of language learning. The suggestions also make connections with the world beyond the classroom and textbook. They lead into the final part of this chapter where you measure your progress.

Inductive v. deductive tasks

Inductive tasks you can set yourself include getting hold of language samples (from magazines, from correspondence you are having on the Internet with penpals) and trying to make up some rules for yourself, based on what you see. An example could be trying to work out (and in some cases revise what you know already) from a piece of prose all the ways of distinguishing between singular and plural or between you (two) and you (all). You can then go to a grammar book and check your intuition. In deductive tasks you do the opposite. These are more like traditional textbook exercises where a rule is given, you apply it and then you look up the key to make sure you are right.

Grade the tasks

If you make the tasks manageable you will have more chance of enjoying them and doing them more often. If your goal is to practise language, set up tasks that are within your capability. The difficulty could be in terms of the language or it could be in terms of the content. Here's an example.

1. Work with four people, taking turns to bring along a photocopied article cut up into paragraphs.
2. Make the content of the article familiar so that you are not struggling at the same time with some entirely new subject. Try to look for newspaper or magazine articles on topics that interest you: sport, travel or even recipes. If you are using recipes, then of course the person preparing the jigsaw has to cut off the numbers.
3. In pairs you try to re-order the paragraphs to make a complete text.
4. Talk about the language clues and the meaning clues that helped you.

Another way of making the task more difficult or easier is to modify the time limits. Can you put the article together in 60 seconds? Watch out for boredom, though. If things are too easy you and your friends will lose interest. There are further ideas on tasks right through this book. We turn now to ways of measuring your progress.

5.2 MEASURING PROGRESS

The traditional way of knowing how you are getting on in your language is to wait for the teacher to return your last test or assignment. In this section we look at some less passive ways of measuring your progress, particularly ways based on the goals you have written.

Assessing your writing

Start by trying to assess your own writing. One of the advantages of assessing your own work is that you are better placed than the teacher to focus on the process rather than on the final product. Ask yourself these questions about your writing:

1. How good am I at getting started?
If the answer is 'terrible' then try to narrow down the problem. Is it the lack of ideas that holds you back or the fact that you simply don't enjoy writing? Maybe you don't think it's important and would rather be spending the time talking. In that case you need to plan some writing tasks that are also sociable (see Chapter 13).

2. Am I making sensible use of resources?
There is a happy medium between sitting thinking up all your ideas in English and then turning to the dictionary for a translation (which is not recommended), and the other extreme, which refuses to use any support. After all, even in our own language we use dictionaries.

3. Am I completing my assigned writing task in a reasonable time?
If not, the answer could be that you are trying to make the versions too perfect, a practice that holds you up from spending time on other aspects of your language development.

4. How much and what types of writing am I doing?
Measure your progress in terms of the amount and types of writing you are doing. Here are some categories:

in-class writing / out-of-class writing,
formal topics / informal topics,

one-off versions / versions edited for improvements,
for yourself to read / for another audience.

This advice applies in particular to writing done for assignments. Try to
get hold of writing from students who have received a high mark.
Compare yours with theirs. What are the differences? Go beyond
counting little mistakes. Look at the wider shape of their writing. Look
too at the teacher's comments on your own writing and on the other
person's. What makes their piece of writing excellent?

Work with other students to give one another feedback on your
writing. Look for some of these points.

How well does the style match the purpose?
Is the length about right?
Are the ideas relevant?
How varied is the language?
How effective are the introduction and conclusion?

Measure progress against goals

Check yourself in relation to the goals you have set. This gives you more
specific insights than waiting to see a mark at the top of a page returned
by the teacher. It turns you from a passive to an active learner. You
realise how much responsibility you have for the progress you do or do
not make. Some books have lists of points to check yourself against but
you can easily use your own specific goals as your check list. Here are
examples for reading and for speaking.

For reading
'In a newspaper I can get the general sense of

headlines
newspaper articles
letters to the editor

without using a dictionary / with minimal use of a dictionary.'

'When reading a chapter in a novel I can tell someone else what the
chapter is about in a couple of sentences.'

For speaking
'My friends and I can talk for five/ten/fifteen minutes on general topics without switching back to English.'
'I can make arrangements with friends/strangers on the phone.
Notice that so far the examples are about whether you can or cannot do something. Another way to self-assess is to say how well you can do something: very fluently, reasonably fluently, with some hesitation, and so on.

Evaluating a language course

So far we have considered ways of measuring your individual progress. Part of this depends on the course you are attending. As the student of Dutch reported in Chapter 1, you may have concerns about the way the course is taught. These days students are usually asked for feedback on their courses. You should take the chance to shape the way the course is taught, and in some cases its content. The evaluation will probably be seen by the teacher and in some cases by the head of department.

What is the purpose of evaluation?

Here are some of the reasons why you should fill in evaluation forms if you have the chance.

Evaluation is not the same thing as seeing how many students passed the course exam or which class had the better marks. In fact, some people think that the teacher who has made some difference to a class that is not doing well shows better teaching skills than the teacher of a top class, all of whom do well. Evaluation is designed to make a difference. It is part of a bigger process of improving teaching and learning in an institution. It is also part of a general trend towards accountability amongst teachers. Teachers are encouraged to take notice of what students write. The more specific your advice is, the more helpful it is to the teacher or to the head of department. At the same time it will help you think in a different way about what you want to know or get from a course and what use you can make of it.

Students ask about the follow-on effects of what they write. Could a teacher be sacked if students give a bad evaluation? Does it make a difference to this course or to the next one? Who follows up on the comments? Students who take the trouble to complete evaluations want to know that the effort has been worthwhile. The answers are different in different institutions, but your student representative should be able to find some answers for you. If the feedback is given during the course then it should make a difference right now, which is not to say that every idea put forward by everyone is attended to. If it is at the end of the course then next year's students benefit just as you benefited from improvements suggested last year.

What do we evaluate?

Course evaluation can focus on any or all of these aspects of the course:

> classroom activities,
> the course materials,
> assessment procedures (including types of assignment).

Apart from the text book, what materials does the teacher provide for learning? What exactly do you do in class? What is the point of these tasks and the homework you are expected to do?

You could be asked to comment on aspects relating to the teacher. This is not the place to make personal remarks. Comments about the lecturers' clothes are likely to stop people from taking the rest of your remarks seriously. Specific questions such as the following could help guide your comments.

> Is the teacher providing clear models of the spoken language?
> Does he or she share talking time with the students?
> Does the teacher's language go beyond what is in the textbook?
> When students ask grammar questions, do the teacher's answers show a good theoretical knowledge *about* the language?
> Are the explanations well structured?
> Is the teacher's written language at a high enough standard for advanced students?

Think about how you would know whether the teacher was doing well in these areas. Would you judge by the person's academic qualifications or by what you saw? How much do you value having a native speaker of the language or a member of your own language group? What difference would it make to you?

Then there is the teacher's classroom management. This topic is a popular one with students. They see good classroom management as a key factor in language learning. Again, these questions could guide you in answering:

Does the teacher organise interesting small group work?
How well does she manage large classes of mixed language proficiency?
Is he good at motivating the students?

How is evaluation organised?

Feedback may be spoken or written; it may be handed directly to the teacher or passed on through the class representative. Open discussion can work well if there is an informal atmosphere and if students do not feel intimidated. In a language class this informal feedback could sound like this:

Could we have more smaller tests instead of one big one?
Could you make us all talk?
Why don't you correct all our mistakes when you mark?
How much of the textbook do you expect us to know for the exams?

Sometimes the teacher is absent during the discussion time and has the results passed on through a student representative. Another way is for students to write down their comments. Although this does not ensure confidentiality, because, after all, the teacher can recognise your handwriting, it does allow you to write things that would be awkward to say in front of your fellow students, such as:

I'd like us to change conversation groups each week.
We have too many take-home tests. How do you know some people don't copy from one another?
Please change the reader. It's boring.

Written feedback may be on a blank piece of paper or on a prepared form which the teacher uses to see how a new idea has gone. For example:

Last week we tried a group activity for encouraging everyone to talk. What did you think about it?

The answers could be multi-choice, ranging from 'Great, give us more,' to 'We all thought it was a waste of time.' You could be asked to rank class activities in order of preference.

Conclusion

This chapter has emphasised the importance of being involved in setting and measuring learning goals. In the next chapter you will see that keeping a learning journal is one way of doing this.

6

KEEPING A LEARNING
JOURNAL

> *Many students are now being encouraged to keep language-learning journals.
> They are a way to reflect on the learning that is happening instead of just waiting
> for the lecturer to tell students how they are progressing. In this chapter the idea
> of a learning journal, which records your language learning and lets you think
> about it, is presented with examples from students. The chapter concludes with the
> journal of one student kept over a period of a few months.*

6.1 DEFINITIONS AND REASONS

Students' views on learning

Some students rely entirely on doing what the lecturer says must be
done to pass the final course exam. If a vocabulary test is coming up they
learn their words in the best way they can. If they have to write an essay
they take their dictionaries, sit at the word-processor and start writing.
Try asking half a dozen people how their language learning is going and
here are some typical answers. The answers are numbered so that we can
examine them in detail.

1. Well, I learned 30 new words this week.
2. I finished the essay on time.
3. I'm doing extra exercises to help my grammar.
4. We did 'Sport and Leisure' this week.
5. My friends and I spoke Chinese for 20 minutes at lunchtime.

You can see immediately that some people, like Student 1, are interested in the *amount of language* they have learned. By 'learned' Student 1 may mean that she has written out and spent some time reciting 30 new words. She may even have tested herself on them. On the other hand she may mean that she scored 100% on a test of those 30 words.

Student 2, on the other hand, thinks of language learning as a series of *tasks* that have to be completed on time. This week he has an essay, next week he needs to prepare a topic so that he can join in a tutorial discussion, and every week he needs to get to his classes on time. He has no say in the type of task set; his role is just to get it done.

Student 3 is one of those conscientious students who set themselves *more of the same tasks* set in class. In this case it is extra exercises, but it could just as well have been sitting in the language laboratory for twice the required time. The principle here is that 'more is better'.

Others, like Student 4, think of language study in terms of topics covered, with 'Sport and Leisure' this week, 'Going to the Theatre' next week, and so on. They may even remember new vocabulary and structures in relation to the textbook chapter where they first appeared.

A few people are like Student 5, who has thought of a way of increasing the amount of time spent actually using the language. Meeting friends at lunchtime is one of many *social strategies* that improve the learning process. Student 5 is planning one of the many strategies available, as we saw in Chapter 3, for improving language learning.

All of the answers given by the students mention something important about language learning. You cannot communicate effectively if you do not have enough words to do it with (1), and however much you enjoy using the language you won't pass the course exam unless your work is handed in so that it can be marked (2). Doing extra of the same work is a good idea if you have first sorted out what went wrong with the first exercise (3). It is helpful to be able to picture situations where you will eventually be using the language (4). It is even more important to be thinking for yourself of the activities that will make learning more pleasurable and more effective for you (5).

Why keep a learning journal?

In summary, there are several reasons why keeping a journal is a good idea. It is a way of reflecting in a systematic way on all the things you are currently doing to improve your language learning. It makes you write every day or every week on a variety of topics. Although it is never seen by your friends or corrected by the teacher, it increases your fluency and your accuracy as well as your ability to think in the new language. It also helps you understand more about the learning process, which may in turn make a difference to your attitude towards learning. If you are past the beginners' stage, you could even try writing your journal in the new language.

The reasons students mention for keeping learning journals can be summarised under three headings. They help your actual language development, they help the process of study, and they can make a positive difference to your attitude.

Language reasons

The language reasons apply only if you are keeping the journal in the new language. If you are still at the early stages, then try writing the first part in the new language and then switch to your own language to express more complex ideas. Gradually the portions written in the foreign language will increase, which is good for your motivation. Here are the ways you will notice your language improving through your entries.

1.   Forcing yourself to write at a reasonable speed without constantly checking the dictionary for the right word will increase your *fluency*. You will gradually overcome the feeling that 'I can't get started', which you can sometimes have in writing a formal essay.

2.   You will find that you can *use a few words to say plenty*, just as little children speaking in their own language make the words they know do the work of the many they have still to learn. Children hardly ever withdraw from a conversation with adults just because they cannot find the exact word that adults might use. For example (and the examples will all be in English), you can express an idea in simpler words, so that 'computer based resources' becomes 'lists of books on the computer'. You can use concrete words instead of abstract. Instead of 'the teaching staff,' write 'the teachers'. You can also express ideas in less complex sentence structures if you have to, so that instead of writing: 'I find that it's difficult to follow when other people speed up their talk during tutorials,' you can write, 'People speak fast in class. I can't understand them.'

3. Thinking about the way to express yourself also improves the *accuracy* of your new language as you search your memory for the best word to use in the middle of a sentence. The word you find may well be one at the front of your mind because you have just started to learn it, which means you are constantly recycling new vocabulary, instead of putting it aside until you need it for translation or an essay.

4. You are also practising a wider *range of sentence structures* than you would need for a formal exercise. As soon as you read or hear a new sentence pattern you can make a point of starting to use it in your learning journal.

5. Finally, you are thinking about 'grammar' at a higher level than single sentences as you join one idea to the next. Just as, in conversations, people have to link their ideas to the remarks already made by others, so writers need to *connect ideas* to one another. Although a journal entry is not the same as a formal essay, it still requires some links between one idea and the next as well as between today's entry and earlier ones. As you join the ideas you will be using phrases such as these:

Another reason . . .
That reminds me to . . .
In short . . .

It also introduces introductory remarks such as

Three good things happened to my language study this week.
I want to think about why I had a low test mark today.

Ideas

1. Putting ideas into words *clarifies your own thinking* about how you are studying. This is different from needing time to find the right words. As one student wrote:

I like writing better than speaking because I can have time to think.

Keeping a journal allows you to say something, then correct yourself or add an idea until the thought you are trying to express becomes clear, just as ideas become clearer to you in your own language when you try to put them into words.

2.   When you glance back at your journal you can see which topics you are mentioning frequently and which you are leaving out. For example, as you spell out details of the strategies you are using to improve your study you may notice that they are all to do with organisation and none of them relate to actual thinking. This could lead to *extending your strategies*.

3.   Having to search for new topics to write about each week (or twice weekly) *broadens the number of topics* you are thinking about in the new language. These could include cultural aspects of language use.

4.   *Journal writers become creative* in their thinking as one idea leads to another. If you don't put a time limit on your journal writing you can simply keep going until the ideas run out.

5.   Writers find themselves *exploring topics in more depth* than when they just toss off remarks in speaking. You don't have to worry about leaving time for the other person to say something.

Attitudinal reasons

1.   In writing a journal you are *taking some responsibility for your own learning* as you

identify your own strengths and weaknesses,
plan ways of overcoming weaknesses,
decide what to do about parts of the course that you find boring,
report discussions with other students about their study habits.

2.   Your *confidence increases* as you find you *can* write a whole page without having to stop all the time. This is in contrast to classroom language use, such as speaking in front of others. If you are a naturally shy person you may feel either that you don't have much to say, or that you have the ideas but not the language for expressing them. Keeping a regular learning journal can show you that neither of these things is true. Everyone has ideas and everyone can express them in some way at each level of language learning.

What can you write ab

Just as a personal journal re   f your
general life, so a language-lea   s, your
concerns and your plans for learning. In the last chapter we considered
some of the strategies used by successful language learners. Here are
some more detailed suggestions.

1   Write about how you organise your learning

Organisational strategies are the ones that come to mind most easily (see
Chapter 3). They include all the things you do to make the actual study
process easier, from tidying your bedroom so that you can find your
books, to working out how to use the various computer-based resources
in the library. However, there are many more organisational strategies
than these two examples waiting to be tried out. Here are a few reported
by successful language learners.

> I watch videos and see movies a lot now. I really enjoy them. Although I
> don't understand the conversation at all I still know the meaning.

> The words I don't know make me stop talking. It's difficult to explain things
> to other people if I have many words I don't know. So I have a notebook
> and collect words I use often. I try to use new words because when I learn
> new words in my text but don't have a chance to use them, I forget them
> quickly.

Two other examples of organising your learning are to borrow videos
and to work out the best way of keeping a vocabulary notebook.

2   Summarise your week's learning

Putting into words what you have learned helps you have a sense of
progress. You can organise your summary in any way you like. Look
back at the five students at the start of this chapter. You could mention
your progress in terms of the things you can now do for the first time or
do better:

> *After listening to the dialogue several times I now have a better idea of the
> difference between greeting people formally and greeting friends.*

Another way to summarise the week could be by topic and the task that went with it.

> *This week I read an article about inoculations, we had a class discussion about the role of the United Nations and I wrote a summary of a short story by a nineteenth-century writer.*

The most traditional way of recording the week's work would be to imitate Student 1 and record the number of new words and new structures you have learned and revised:

> *This week I learned —— new words from the textbook and added – words to my notebook from other reading.*
> *In tutorials we practised using a new grammatical structure.*

3 Note problems

The journal is a place to be absolutely honest about aspects of your language learning that are not going well. Perhaps you understand the new language when you read it but have problems writing, or vice versa. Two students report their weaknesses.

> I want to change my accent but it's very difficult. Also I don't know how to change it.

> When I talk to someone face to face, I understand. But I don't understand native-speaker friends because they use a lot of words. Also a conversation is too fast.

Talking about problems is a familiar way of making them manageable. Your journal can be a form of self-talk:

> *Recently I can't enjoy anything because I'm always worrying about my [language]. I feel nervous every day.*
> *Today was a good day but now I am too tired to write in my journal so I should go to bed early.*

4 Suggest solutions

Along with the problems, see if you can think of ways of solving some of them. Try starting like this:

Maybe I should look for help from . . .
I noticed that X . . .   That's something I could try.
One of my learning problems is . . .   Maybe if I . . .
One of the other students said that . . .

Four students made these suggestions to themselves:

> Sometimes when I can't understand the words I try to guess.

> I think if I want to speak the language very well I must speak it more.

> Sometimes I don't know the right words when I am talking. I explain by gestures and saying 'for example'.

> I think my vocabulary is too weak so I have to focus on my new words.

5 Note new ways of learning

When you hear a good tip from someone else, and you think, 'That's a great idea. I must try it,' you can note that in your journal. Then the following week you can take the process one step further by thinking about how it has worked. The journal can express your feelings about the strategy and note your suggestions for changing things next time round. The first time you try something out it may not work because of the way you have organised it. Think 'aloud' in the journal about how you could try it a second time.

> *I tried a new way of recording vocabulary today. I . . . but next time I think I would . . .*

6 Describe your goals

Your course will have certain broad goals, and so will you, as we saw in the last chapter. Put them into words as encouragement, as this student has in relation to his career.

> I need reading skills because I want to be a translator but it is difficult.

The learning journal is also the place to be specific. Notice how this student makes a connection between writing and speaking:

I want to write long sentences in Russian. I think if I could write long sentences then I would be able to speak very well.

7 Mention your strengths

Another form of encouragement is thinking of what you do well, like this student who writes about how he worked at making one of his language strengths even more successful:

> I think I'm better at listening than at writing and reading. And now I've got a small radio and I try to listen to it. It's quite hard for me but I think it's pretty good practice too.

8 Ask questions

Finally, pose questions which you can follow up later. Try noting at the same time where you could go for solutions, as shown in Table 6.1.

9 Be specific

If you are wanting ideas to get you started on a diary, here are some specific areas of language that you could write about.

Your writing
　　How do you prepare to write essays?
　　Are there any other ways you could experiment with?
　　How can you make use of the teachers' written feedback?
　　What are your main strengths?
　　Which areas of writing do you need to develop?

TABLE 6.1

Question	Source of Answers
How do other people remember so many words?	Ask them.
Is there such a thing as easy language readers?	Try the library.
I wonder what progress I *really* am making?	Keep results.
What's the answer to shyness?	Watch others.

Your reading
   What are your main sources of reading?
   Are there any other sources you could follow up?
   What is most difficult about reading textbooks?
   What tactics do you have for remembering what you read?
   What exactly do you hope to get out of your reading?

Your listening
   How do you make yourself concentrate while you listen?
   What is the most difficult aspect of listening to another language?
   How are your note-taking skills?
   What do you do about listening during small group discussions?
   How do you react when you don't understand?

Your speaking
   Which aspect of your speaking is most successful?
   How is your contribution in small groups?
   What stops you from contributing? (What could you do about it?)

All of these ideas are expanded in Part II of the book.

6.2 A LANGUAGE LEARNER'S JOURNAL

For the second part of this chapter you will be reading the journal extracts of a beginner learner interspersed with comments. This person was a language teacher herself, and therefore had insights into her learning from two perspectives: teaching and learning. She lived thousands of miles from the country where the language was spoken. It was her ancestral language and she had managed to find a native speaker as a private tutor. She made use of books and tapes in between lessons. Even if you are a classroom learner there should be parallels here with your own progress.

AFTER LESSON ONE

Student–teacher cooperation

   Here are the things the tutor did which gave me a sense of having some say in the lesson.

1. She let me take along my own book and gave the impression of liking it.
2. She did what I asked on the first lesson, namely reading the dialogues aloud and letting me imitate her.
3. She praised my attempts to pronounce the words.
4. She made it clear she would enjoy working with me.

This student was fortunate to find a tutor who was willing to share the role of lesson planner. The student had an idea of how the lessons should start. These were modified later but at the beginning that is what she wanted. Notice too how important the affective aspects of learning are. You are fortunate if you have a teacher who is good at mentioning your strengths.

The learner's part

Active learning is important at any stage of the process but some beginners think they can't do anything about their progress. This is not the case, as the next journal entry shows.

Here are some of the things I found I could do for myself after the first lesson.

1. I went over the pronunciation straight away when I got home.
2. I combed through the lessons for words and phrases I could use to write letters to people. That was better than a conversation for the meantime because who would wait for the next bit of the conversation while I went looking through the book?
3. I wrote little things in a notebook. They were just sentences that I wrote without looking anything up, to test myself to see how much I could say.
4. I read the grammar rules, which were explained in English.

So far I haven't done any grammar exercises because it's too exciting being able to write real things, but I think I'll get around to doing some grammar exercises soon so that some of the patterns will fix themselves in my head.

All of this was written after the first lesson. Notice how she combines getting straight on to genuine communication through writing letters with taking a systematic approach to grammar. There is no reason why you shouldn't combine both, as this learner did. Communicating in whatever way works best is a way of keeping yourself motivated even at this early stage.

AFTER LESSON TWO

Some new ideas.

1. Listening to a record of singing in Welsh and following the words on paper.
2. Writing letters to the teacher. (The teacher was good enough to write one back.) A lesson from the book now translates itself into genuine communication at however puerile a level. Receiving a letter back was a tremendous boost to the efforts.

Writing the letter still means tailoring what I can say to the language I have already learned. In other words, the medium is to a certain extent determining the message.

Fitting the message to the language available

In the first excitement of language learning it doesn't seem to matter that the communication is driven more by the medium than the message. This is particularly true if you are learning a foreign language in your own country, where you have the safety of being yourself most of the day. It doesn't matter if you feel slightly childish just for a while. If you go abroad to study, then the needs of everyday life take over and it becomes tiring not to sound like the mature person you normally are.

Singing

Notice that this learner mentions music and singing as important in the early lessons. As you will see later in the book, even advanced students enjoy learning through song. It has two big advantages, one being that you can relax more and the other that repetition is a normal part of singing, so you can say the same simple refrain a number of times without being asked to move on.

AFTER LESSON THREE

Planning independent tasks

If the learning time is to be extended beyond the short lesson time each week, then learners have to think up tasks for themselves to do between the times with the teacher. In this case the learner has thought up a dictation-type task for herself. She listens to the songs and then tries to take down the words.

> I now have the tape of the songs to play for myself at home, plus some of the words. The next step will be to transcribe the words of the others.

Comprehension

Very soon meaning takes over, to the learner's surprise. Notice how quickly her systematic learning of vocabulary brings results.

> The third lesson is reading the next chapter for pronunciation and meaning. I could hardly believe that I could actually understand some of the content from the context, having learned some of the words and phrases in earlier lessons.

Memorising

At the same time as working on comprehension, the learner is attending to memorising. In Chapter 4 we discussed the opinion that there isn't much point in learning chunks of language by heart. An opposite viewpoint is expressed by some students, who find that it helps them. For one thing they have the sounds of the language going over and over in their mind and for another it gives them phrases that they can use later instead of working down at the word level.

Receptive and productive language

All of us, even in our own language, understand far more than we can say. You can test this out by listening to a detailed discussion on a technical subject you can only just understand but couldn't put into words for yourself.

> I still cannot respond properly in a genuine conversation even about simple things, but I was able to recite off large chunks of the dialogue from the previous lesson, which I had memorised. The teacher took one part and I took the other. She had to prompt me and correct me in one or two places but she was kind enough to express praise too. I see that praise is important even for the enthusiastic learner.

Authentic communication

At the early stages of language learning there is a pull between wanting to have genuine communication and not being able to do it yourself or not finding people who are patient enough to listen or read and respond.

> I am trying to write more 'letters' in my exercise book from which I can copy sentences later into real letters when people start replying to my earlier letters. The earlier ones were not really interesting enough to prompt people into replying immediately.

SEVERAL LESSONS LATER

Vocabulary growth

With her letter writing the student found that the more words you know the more interesting your messages are. There is no substitute for solid study of vocabulary.

> The weekly letters to the teacher now come nearer to being able to say what I want without having to start with what I know how to say and then working the message around it.
>
> It becomes more and more possible to say a wide number of things by using general nouns and verbs instead of the more specific ones I would be using in English. Adding the same few adjectives allows me to express broad categories. For instance, the word 'good' is used for delicious (food) attractive (garden), pleasant (teacher) and so on. If one is willing to give away the adult bit, then it is possible to be quite expressive.

Language input

The diary continues.

> The main sources of input are
>
> > The textbook.
> > Extra reading material.
> > Recorded songs with tapescripts and translations.
> > A tape from which I understand some phrases and from which I list phrases as I think I know them. On the tape a man is recounting his childhood.
> > The dictionary which I look up when I'm writing a letter and want to find a word to say something. (This is probably the least satisfactory way, because it's an old dictionary I cannot tell whether the word is in current usage.)

Students (and their teachers) give plenty of thought to the sources of language that they are exposed to. Usually there is a combination of authentic sources (materials for native speakers) and materials designed for language learners. In this case the extra reading material was a magazine for children, which could be ordered from overseas. While the content was, understandably, more childish than the student's usual reading, the incentive of being able to understand some of the articles overcame that barrier. The tape, on the other hand, was much more difficult. It had been recorded on radio and sent to the tutor by relatives. The strategy of writing down only the phrases she knew gave the learner a sense of progress although she didn't really have an understanding of the overall meaning.

The tutor's role

It seems to me that the teacher has quite a part to play in providing some motivation. Although the urge to learn must come from within, there is no doubt that being congratulated on one's progress is a great support.

Learners don't often have the chance to choose their own teachers, but if they do, they should look out for one who is encouraging.

A MONTH LATER

Resources

It's not always easy to re-find something you know you have learned. Sometimes you'll remember the book where you read it but you still have the problem of finding it. Not all books are well indexed or indexed in the way that is most helpful.

That leads on to the thought of what is the best way of recording information for future reference. I use a dictionary arranged alphabetically, or rather two forms of a dictionary, one from Welsh to English and the second vice versa. I prefer the former because it makes me use the language more, but of course if you have no memory of the word at all then that doesn't work.

When you are choosing a grammar reference book or a textbook, one quality to look for is accessibility. There are more ideas for organising your vocabulary learning in the next chapter.

Creating a context for language practice

After reading a story I sometimes try to retell it, either to myself as I'm walking down the road, or to my teacher. A teacher must need to be really dedicated to listen to the badly rehashed version of a story that may not have interested her in the first place.

Even when the audience was someone who already knew the story, she played an important role in giving some point to the retelling.

Remembering and using new words

I've noticed something about the words I use to retell the story. If I've only recently read the story I don't seem to incorporate the new words in the retelling. I still seem to use simpler paraphrases.

e.g. 'He didn't do good things' for 'He was causing trouble.'

It seems as if the new words do not automatically become part of the productive vocabulary although the process must be happening slowly because words that keep recurring in stories do seem to come out in my talking and writing.

This learner's experience with trying to recall all words is exactly what researchers say. We need to meet words many, many times in context before they are fixed in our minds to the point where we can recall them when they are needed.

Simplified readers

Using the simplified reader specially prepared for language learners gives a tremendous sense of progress. By the third story I was actually under-standing the broad meaning even without having to go to the index. On about the third reading I start noting words that I think I'd like to use.

Readering books that take adult themes but retell them in simplified language provide an incentive to keep reading. These may be versions of literature or folk stories or biographies or other non-fiction.

Recycling the language

I do two kinds of writing. One is letter writing when my first aim now is to say what I want to say. The second kind is what I'd call language practice.

> That means I deliberately use new words or constructions which have come up in the textbook or in my reading.

The comments here show that sentence patterns as well as new words need to be used in real contexts if they are to be learned properly.

Assessing learning

We think of a teacher as the one who tells learners how they are getting on, but as we saw in Chapter 5, the learner needs to be able to do some assessing too. The assessment can include *how* you are learning as well as *how much*.

> Right now (Is it 3 months after starting?) I find myself learning more from reading than from the textbook, but that might be just a stage. The textbook is good for summarising verb tenses and for explaining points idiosyncratic to Welsh.

SIX WEEKS LATER

The ups and downs of progress

> The proverbial plateau through June, followed by a surge of development this month. I am becoming increasingly interested in affective factors such as motivation, occasions for language use and other people's expectations. For example, the arrival of a letter in Welsh is an incentive, as is the opportunity to share a book with someone or exchange correspondence. The chance for a singing performance was an extra boost.

It is unrealistic to expect that the surge of progress at the beginning will be kept up over the months. In this case music provided an injection of interest. At some point in the lessons the tutor's husband offered to play the piano while the student and tutor sang songs. This provided an interesting break from the intensity of the lessons while giving the chance to practise pronunciation.

Organisational strategies

Part of the organisation for learning is to make information accessible to yourself.

The need to systematise the learning surfaces from time to time. I try to organise lists of frequently used verbs in the past. My dictionary is organised in two ways, L1 to L2 and vice versa. Then I had the idea of topic vocabulary lists so that I could find words faster. Finding words that have been met once and half remembered is one of the biggest pitfalls.

Another part of organisation involves getting hold of resources, particularly those that go beyond the textbook.

You really start to crack the code when you find yourself trying to read material not written for language learners. I have been doing this with a magazine of local news items, which have little intrinsic interest for me but which are a fascinating way of reading little bits and pieces of news about other people in villages far away, the very people, in fact, who are speaking the language I'm learning.

Analysis of progress

As noted earlier, it is important, from time to time, to stand back and take stock of your progress. What am I doing well? What needs further work? This learner, like most, swings between pleasure in the things she can do and attention to those she can't.

My biggest lack is still in not being able to sustain a normal conversation. Anything I can say is still determined by the words I know rather than by the ideas in my head.

Making the best of resources

I have tried, parallel with using the main textbook written for adult learners, to work on a structured course for children. It works on principles of dialogue for input and contextualised drills for practice. I do it as a means of systematising my learning rather than through interest in the children's doings.

TWO MONTHS LATER

The affective factor again

I am constantly amazed at the effect of praise and admiration for my efforts on the part of my teacher and her husband. I would have thought that my motivation to learn the language was enough of a goad to further efforts and that as an adult learner I could progress without the encouragement of

others. Instead, I find my efforts doubling each time either of them con-
gratulates me on progress.

Using the telephone

Telephone talk is usually considered much more difficult than talking
face to face because all of the clues such as facial expression and gestures
are missing from the other person.

> One great step forward came when the teacher suggested in one of her
> weekly letters that I should try ringing her and speaking nothing but Welsh
> for a few sentences. Before ringing I tried some 'immersion' tactics. I
> played my Welsh songs, did some reading and wrote some letters. I also
> started going over useful words, but did not actually write out a script
> although I had planned some ideas.
>   We managed to continue talking for about five minutes, my enthusiasm
> balanced by extremely ungrammatical speech and one or two re-wordings
> when I could sense that my story was not being understood.

Being aware of the other person's reaction is very important in any
conversation. When there's a problem, you can re-word the idea, provided the listener indicates non-understanding.

> All that is written about having to make a choice between fluency and
> accuracy when thrust into a genuine conversation when one very much
> wants to say something rather than practise language, was true in this case.
> Rules that I 'knew' were broken, familiar words forgotten, all in the
> interests of holding my listener's attention.

These comments highlight a phenomenon that many learners notice.
They can get exercises right when nothing depends on it, but when a
whole lot of factors come into play in a real conversation then things are
not so easy. The time factor is crucial. Most people want to finish a
sentence in reasonable time, especially when someone is waiting to hear
it. The ideas move faster than the language and, of course, you are
taking part in a dialogue, not making a speech, so the other person's
contributions have to be taken into account.

6.3 SUMMARY OF ADVICE

Based on the learner's diary and the commentary on it, here is a
summary of advice.

1. Learners have just as important a part to play in progress as do their teachers.

2. Stand back and reflect on your learning from time to time.

3. When reviewing your progress, think about successful areas as well as those that need working on.

4. All aspects of learning can make a difference to progress: organisation, mental attitude, and feelings.

5. It is normal to have times when you don't seem to be making much progress.

6. It helps to have a range of language input.

PART II
STRATEGIES FOR LANGUAGE ACQUISITION

7

VOCABULARY LEARNING

> *Some people think of vocabulary learning as writing down words in a notebook, covering over one column and trying to remember the words from the other column. The stages we'll be considering are: finding the new words, working out their meanings in various ways, recording words in formats that are helpful to you, finding ways of remembering them, checking your recall of the words and, at the same time, starting to use them.*

In this second half of the book we apply the general ideas from Part I to more specific topics, starting with vocabulary learning. For example, in Chapter 3 we looked at strategies of successful language learners. Now let's get specific. What do successful language learners say about how they learn vocabulary? As an active language learner you can play a part in the six stages of vocabulary growth: finding words, understanding their meaning, recording them, remembering them, testing your recall and, of course, using them.

7.1 FINDING NEW WORDS

Planning your sources

It may seem unnecessary to talk about where you will find the words for your language learning. Surely they will be provided in the textbook or class handouts? The more successful you want to be, not only to get good grades in your course but also to use the language orally and in reading and writing, the more you will want to go beyond the supplied materials. It is up to you to search out words from many sources, developing your own hunting plan. Successful language learners report these sources.

Words/phrases that I hear my teacher or someone else use.

Extra readings in the text.

Conversing with native speakers.

Cassettes with songs and the words, listened to often and memorised a couple of songs.

The general pattern in their suggestions is that they looked for words in a context rather than in word lists, although of course they often organised the words into lists of their own later.

How many new words a week?

The decision about how many new words you want to learn per week is important in relation to your final target. You could, of course, decide on the target first and then divide it up. Here is some information that may help you set your target.

Do you know how many words six-year-olds know in their first language? As mentioned earlier, many estimates from studies around the world suggest that children probably know 2,000 words by the time they are six. From then on they add between 1,000 and 2,000 words a year. If you do some calculations you'll see what your weekly target needs to be (see Figure 7.1).

What sort of words?

As well as deciding how many, you need to think of which words you need and at what level. We all understand more words than we can use. We hear the words in context and we understand them, but we may not

---

How many words do you want to learn a week?   ____

Multiply this number by the weeks you will be studying, to find your total vocabulary goal for the year.   ____

FIGURE 7.1

need to use them ourselves. It could help to mark separately words you want to understand when they are used in the new language but which you are not going to bother using yourself. These are sometimes called 'receptive' rather than 'active' vocabulary. They could include words you meet in specialist articles in journals or newspapers on particular topics: space exploration, or some area of science which is outside your specialty.

News headlines are an easy source of new vocabulary. Start listing them according to topics in your vocabulary collection. You could use topic headings (disasters, international conferences) or language headings (metaphors, descriptive phrases). If one of your interests in language learning is for translation purposes this collection of current vocabulary will be valuable to you.

7.2 UNDERSTANDING WORD MEANINGS

Once you have found the words, usually in chunks of language such as people's conversations, radio or television programmes, or through various types of reading, the next step is to work out the meaning. It is one thing to understand words at a superficial level when you see or hear them. It takes more understanding to remember them when you need to use them.

One way of remembering words long-term is to work out the meaning for yourself rather than turning straight to the dictionary. It is worth taking what seems like a longer route when you are reading. Some students think this advice is the teacher's way of making things difficult. In fact many studies have shown that thinking deeply about the meaning and trying to work it out is the way to make the words stick.

This guessing or sensible prediction is not as difficult as you might think. If you meet a word often enough in context you start to have a feeling for it. Unconsciously (or consciously if they want to hurry the process up) learners find themselves developing a feeling for word meanings. They are able to categorise words mentally in various ways. They know that this new word usually appears in articles or conversations about such-and-such a topic, and they start to have a feeling for the word's meaning.

Try yourself out with the following example. Imagine that the new word which you have just met in your reading is *kuaka*, which is a real word in a language you probably don't know. Your first clue to its area of meaning is the place where you came across it, which in this case was a geographical magazine. All the surrounding words are put in English here, but imagine that they are words you already know in a new language and only *kuaka* is new. By the end of the article you have come across the new word four times, in the following sentences:

We need to think about looking after *kuaka*.
The Department of Conservation believes there could be a black market in *kuaka*.
Large numbers of *kuaka* are being shot and others are being maimed.
These maimed *kuaka* cannot make it all the way back to Siberia and Alaska.

Before turning to the end of the chapter for the translation, try answering the questions below.

What part of speech is the word?
What clues are there to its meaning?
What word family could the word belong to?
What mental picture are you forming?

The process of intelligent guessing is not just for second-language learners. We use it all the time with our first language, when the telephone line is not clear, when the other person mumbles, when a little child explains something with words that are hard to follow, or when someone introduces a very specialised new word in the middle of a conversation. What happens is that the context helps supply the meaning.

Successful students have all sorts of clever ideas for working out new word meanings. Try reading a passage with a friend and exchanging ideas about what the new words might mean and how you know. Use these and other clues:

hints from the title,
the general meaning of the paragraph,
the sentence before and after,
an intelligent guess.

7.3 RECORDING NEW WORDS

As we mentioned in the chapter on memory, the way you work out the meaning initially and the ways you choose to record the new word will make a difference to whether you can remember it later and recall the word at the right moment. Here are some ways students say are useful.

Lists or cards

The most popular way of recording new words is in lists or on cards. In either case, students, when asked to write down their suggestions, recommend organising the words to make it easy to self-test. (See later in this chapter.) Students are divided as to whether it is a good idea to record the English equivalents, but it could depend on your level and the type of word. Words for concrete items such as flowers, trees, clothing or body parts, for instance, or even some abstract terms like fear, embarrassment and excitement, could be best recorded initially through translation. Once you know enough to write a short paraphrase or example in the new language, that is a good idea, because words can be used slightly differently or have different connotations in different languages. On the other hand, some specialised and technical words are probably better recorded with their exact translation.

Some students recommend organising coloured cards according to categories you find useful. Some people find it helps their memory to use colour coding according to the place where they found the word: blue for the textbook, green for computer-lab programs, and so on.

Make up your own mnemonics

A mnemonic is any memory device that works for you. It could be a sentence including a string of new words such as colours or means of transport, with the initial letter spelling a word, like the acronym HOMES, that some people use to remember the names of the Great Lakes of Canada. It could be a rhyme or an association. Beware that the task of making up the memory device doesn't take longer than it would to learn the word another way! The keyword system is one mnemonic that is frequently mentioned in books about vocabulary learning. Here is an explanation of this system.

You find a word in English that helps you think of the new word. The association may be by the sound of the word or the spelling. If you are learning a language like Japanese or Chinese the look of the word will also be rich in associations. These associations probably don't relate to the real meaning of the new word. It's just that there is something unusual or even funny between the two words. For example, try your imagination on this one. What English words sound like the French word *fromage* (cheese)? How could you picture a cheese in connection with the English words 'from' and 'age'? There is no right answer to these questions. It's a case of using your imagination.

Real associations

With some new words you can make real associations. This is particularly the case when some words from the language you are learning have been borrowed into English or when the two languages have a common ancestry. Thus the Italian word "*bianco*" (white) could be remembered by picturing a blank, white piece of paper.

Mindmaps of related words

This is an idea anyone can try out, however unartistic they feel. Draw spiderwebs with a general word like communication in the centre and related words going out from it.

A continuum is a simpler form of mindmap. It can be used to record words that form a sequence, such as:

disturbing ⟷ frightening ⟷ terrifying

Real objects

Some students report labelling everything in the house at the early stage of language learning when they want to memorise basic words for furniture and parts of the building. One said she points to all the objects as she passes them, saying the words aloud.

Draw pictures

The equivalent of real things, which some students use, is pictures. This works well for concrete words, particularly for groups of words at the initial stage, such as types of furniture, family relationships, or shapes.

Put a number beside the object rather than a translation so that you can check yourself again and again on the same pictures.

Make up sentences

The students who say they made up sentences of their own as a way of recording new words are doing several things at once. They are writing complete sentences they can use later. They also give themselves the chance to try the words out in several forms (singular/plural, different verb tenses) and they are reminding themselves that words have meaning only in a wider context.

7.4 REMEMBERING NEW WORDS

When you think of remembering the new words you have learned in your course you may be thinking only about remembering them for a vocabulary test. That is one kind of remembering. When someone gives you a prompt, such as a paragraph with missing words, you can fill the gap. Another kind of remembering involves finding that word or phrase just at the moment when you need it in the middle of a sentence of your own, such as in the middle of an essay. As already mentioned, it seems that this kind of remembering works well when you have attended effectively to the other two stages, understanding the meaning and recording the words in helpful ways.

Here are students' suggestions for remembering.

Use body language to remember the verbs.

I visualised words and made correspondences with English.

I learn vocabulary by association with pictures, sounds or English words wherever possible.

Point to objects.

Rote learning was suggested by some. This seems to work for lists of words such as numbers and colours. Others used the technique of writing and memorising the original sentences they made up for their vocabulary records. Several students stressed the importance of repetition in meaningful contexts, such as singing songs with the new words in them. Here are three more ideas.

Word grouping

Some ideas for remembering new words can be combined with learning with friends. For example, here is a revision idea which forces you to use the new words as you talk about their shades of meaning.

1. Find a group of 4 students.
2. Put a collection of cards with single words on them in a pile. These could be the word cards you and your friends have already made as part of your recording system.
3. Take turns to select a card each.
4. When they have all been picked up, each pair groups their words. The challenge is to have no fewer than three in a pile and to be able to justify the connection between them. The groups can be very broad. For example:

   All these words have something to do with outdoors.

   Or you can be more specific, as in:

   Our piles are divided into words to do with eating, travelling and looking, etc.

   If you are revising words all from the same source, and therefore the same topic, you can be even more specific. For instance, words from a passage describing a landscape could be divided up like this:

   The groups are as follows: words of colour, place, movement ...

5. The other pairs of students have to guess at the basis for each group.
6. Change piles and make quite different groupings.

Once you have done this activity you will probably think of variations such as forcing yourself to speak in the new language.

Bingo

You can use any children's version of Bingo but speak in the language you are learning. Alternatively you can make your own version with your vocabulary cards. Some supermarket advertisements that are arranged in small squares can be cut up and used for the same purpose.

Exchange learning ideas

Organise a list of words that you and others are finding it hard to remember. Each person in a group is allotted a number of words and brings along one novel idea for remembering them.

7.5 SELF-TESTING

The real test of whether you know a word is whether you can use it appropriately in your talking and writing. More artificial ways are: testing yourself with individual words, with sentences, and with longer passages of text. Many of the ideas already suggested for recording and remembering words actually test your memory and understanding at the same time. If you want to check your progress more formally, then there are several things you can do.

Isolated words

The most common method is to use your original word lists, covering one column. To do this you need to have separated the columns so that you can cover either the translation or the example or the original word. For cards, have the new term on one side and a picture, the translation or a phrase on the other.

Word association

See how many words you can write in a chain of association from one word in your latest vocabulary list.

Words in sentences

If you are making up sentences, then the new words need to be listed in a column that can be covered or folded over, as in Table 7.1. The spacing allows you to cover over the new word as you try to recall it in context.

Here's a variation on gap-filling that can work even at the early stages of language learning. Write out a simple paragraph within the

TABLE 7.1

Sentence	New Word
I notice you've been——. Have a lozenge.	coughing
How long have you had that rasping——?	cough
Sorry about this——. My cold won't go away.	cough
She——all night. That's why her throat is sore.	coughed

word limit you have reached so far but leaving out every fifth word. Then pass it to a friend and take turns to complete each other's paragraphs.

Words in longer passages

If you have found a number of new words in one passage, try this idea for checking your recall after you have tried learning them.

1. Photocopy the passage.
2. White out the new words.
3. Photocopy this new version.
4. Leave it for a day or two.
5. Try writing out the missing words on another page.
6. Check with the original passage.
7. Keep the two pages for later review.

7.6 USING NEW WORDS IN NATURAL LANGUAGE

We now come to the final stage in the learning process. For most language learners in natural (non-classroom) settings, using the word spontaneously is the final step in knowing it. In formal learning you can hurry this process up by starting to use the new words even when you are not forced to as part of an exercise. Many learners reported using new words mentally by way of practice or finding people to talk with. Practising with a friend is often reported by language students.

One student pointed out what can happen when you don't keep using new language.

Regularly go over all the materials previously covered as sometimes when you've moved on a bit you can find you have forgotten the basic stuff through lack of use.

As well as talking, you can set yourself writing tasks. The idea of journals or diaries has already been explored in Chapter 6. Another test is to write a passage using as many as possible of the new words you have learned in a week. In your effort to fit them all in you could finish up with an entertaining piece of writing to exchange with a friend who is doing the same thing. The final step is using the words in speaking and writing.

Summary

Although the ideas in this chapter have been set out in six separate steps, you will have realised that in fact the steps overlap. Trying to work out the meaning for yourself helps you remember the word. Recording the word in interesting ways helps with retrieving it later. Using the words in meaningful situations is a way of remembering them.

To make the ideas in this chapter your own, start trying them out. As you work at some of them you may find that other good ideas come to mind which suit your particular style of learning. Look back at the information in Chapter 3 for some prompts. If rhythm is important to you, try putting the words into sentences that you can set to music. If you learn well through visual images then experiment with interesting pictures and diagrams for recording new words. Whatever tactics you select, words are just the tools with which you read, write, speak and listen. The following chapters take these ideas further in each of these aspects.

*   *   *

Answer to the puzzle: *Kuaka* is the Maori word for 'godwit'.

8

LISTENING TO A NEW LANGUAGE

Listening is the invisible part of language learning. You can see people turning the pages of the books they read, you can hear them talk, you can watch them writing and see what they write but you cannot observe listening. You can only observe the results of it. In this chapter we see what successful language learners have to say about listening in language learning.

The chapter starts with a report of what is involved in learning to listen in a new language. Then there are several examples of opportunities for listening reported by successful language learners. Finally we consider different types of listening that can be done, including ways of making yourself an active listener.

8.1 THE LISTENING PROCESS

What is involved in listening?

When people try to describe what it is that students have to do as they listen to a new language, they come up with several elements. These include listening for words that are recognisable, understanding the meaning of sentences or shorter utterances in a particular context, and remembering the separate parts of what they hear long enough to make sense. Of course if listening also calls for a response, then even more elements are involved. Each of these is a complex process which is closely linked with all the other aspects of language learning.

Recognising words depends on having a growing vocabulary, as we saw in the last chapter. If the words are there in your mind then at least you have a chance of recognising them when someone else says them. If you have learned your vocabulary in sense groups rather than in some arbitrary way such as alphabetical lists, then listening for meaning will be even easier. You also have to recognise the particular meaning the word is likely to have on this occasion. In all languages words take on different meanings or shades of meaning according to the context. Keep the bigger picture of the topic in mind at the same time as noticing individual words. This is easier when someone is giving a prepared talk, such as on the radio, than it is in a conversation, when people go off at tangents all the time, dragging in all sorts of different topics ('That reminds me . . .' 'On another topic . . .' 'Just to get away from that subject for a minute . . .').

When it comes to making sense of utterances it is tempting to try and take the sentence apart and think about all the bits. In reality, there usually isn't time for this, unless you are prerecording and replaying a tape. More useful is trying to listen to longer and longer chunks of language or trying to predict what might be coming next. You can practise this with a tape-recorder too, pressing 'pause' and telling yourself what could be coming next. As you predict and keep on listening you are constantly adjusting your understanding. You might have thought, as one listener did, that everyone else was talking about a battle from World War II whereas in fact the topic was capital punishment.

Part of making sense of what people say involves knowing what their intention is. It is sometimes tricky with another language to know whether someone is trying to entertain you or tell you something tragic, which makes it difficult even to have the right expression on your face. Irony is another thing that's hard to pick up. Perhaps you don't understand whether the person is asking a question or making a statement or a complaint or anything else. Say, for example, you have heard the words 'about 5 o'clock' but nothing else. In that case it is a good idea to say something like this: 'Are you asking me or telling me?'

One problem is that, unlike the process with your own language, it is such an effort to remember the bit before last so as to make sense of what you heard last. There is no short cut to this. It's partly a matter of time and partly a matter of being relaxed about the bits you miss. It is also important not to try and remember the actual words spoken. What is important is the meaning. Think of a parallel in your own language. When you get off the phone to a friend and someone immediately asks,

'What did she have to say?' you paraphrase what you heard rather than repeating the exact words. This happens because you put the new information into your mind alongside everything else you know about the speaker, the events she is describing and so on.

What makes for successful listening?

Good listening depends on a number of factors which you can measure yourself against. General intelligence seems to make a difference. As a student of languages you have probably demonstrated intelligence already. Another is your memory. As explained above, listening involves a good memory, so that anything you do to improve your memory in general will also improve your listening. There are also other, quite specific factors: your background knowledge, your involvement, your interest in the topic and your relationship with the speaker.

I   Background knowledge

When you are listening to something, such as a conversation, a talk or a play, the more you know about the topic the better. Before going to see a play, find out something about the story. This needn't be enough to spoil the plot but just enough to fill in some of the background information without which you might spend the first half wondering what on earth it's all about. One example of failing to have the right background knowledge happened when one person invited another to a party at her home at 'twenty to four'. This seemed a very strange time to the listener, who assumed she had misheard. However much she re-checked, the answer always came back the same. The party was to be at twenty to four. In the end it came down to knowing that the speaker worked at a factory where the workers would be finishing at 3.30 and would be walking straight round the corner to the party.

2   Getting involved

The student's involvement in listening plays an important part. If you put together all the activities that students report for their listening, you could arrange them on a continuum according to how active the listener is, as shown in Figure 8.1.

Here are some practical suggestions for getting involved as a listener.

Passive listening	More active listening	Interactive listening
← -- →		
Listening to songs as you drive along in the car	Singing along	Stopping the tape to think about the meaning

FIGURE 8.1 DEGREES OF INVOLVEMENT IN LISTENING

Keep indicating your understanding. Part of the listening process is to let the other person know how much you have understood. Even saying something that turns out to be irrelevant allows the other person to say, 'Just a minute. That's not what I meant.' Ignoring the other speaker's utterance and carrying on with what you think the topic is, is a common phenomenon in language listening. That is better than silence, which can be mistaken for understanding.

Use body language too, as appropriate to the culture. Shoulder-shrugging, head-shaking, and laughter all form part of active listening and act as signals of understanding or the opposite. An absence of these should be a signal to the speaker. The more vague your signals are, the harder they are to interpret. Saying 'yes, hm . . .' a few times could mean anything.

Picking up one or two words or phrases from the speaker and then echoing them is a way of indicating different meanings. Depending on the intonation, this could mean:

Isn't that amazing?
I agree with you.
That can't be true.
What do you mean?

Re-wording the other person's message gives even more clues about your understanding and keeps the conversation going. For example:

Speaker: Plenty of people can't swim.
Listener: That's true. Many can't.

3   Choosing topics that interest you

Your interest in the topic is important too. Of course you can't force yourself to be interested in every topic that you have to listen to, but when it comes to out-of-class listening, exercise some choice. If you have a choice of tapes in the language laboratory go for those where the topics are stimulating to you. Select radio broadcasts or television programmes on topics you like. These need not be related to your studies.

4 Your relationship with the speaker

Finally, your relationship with the speaker makes a difference to your listening. This is due partly to you and partly to the other person. We all pay more attention to someone who interests us, either in a pleasant or in an unpleasant way. The speaker, in turn, will respond by communicating better if you seem to be involved.

8.2 OPPORTUNITIES TO LISTEN

Successful language learners mention many opportunities for practising listening within a language course, but their answers to the question about what they do to improve their listening show that they also go a step further than the minimum provided. They start by referring to opportunities in class, then to out-of-class opportunities within the school or university, and finally to opportunities further afield.

In-class opportunities

Within their language classes they mentioned these opportunities:

Lectures delivered in the foreign language

By the second or third year of a course you could find yourself listening to lectures on linguistics or literature in the target language. At first this is difficult. It's hard enough to get the gist of what is being said, but taking notes at the same time is even harder. One way to help yourself is to be sure beforehand of what the topic is, by looking at your course outline, and then to read something from the textbook to alert yourself to likely topics. We call this 'providing yourself with a framework for gaining new knowledge'.

Class listening exercises

You may be given dictations in class or you may be asked to listen to something and then respond to it in some way. The language laboratory is the place where you do individual listening practice. Unlike the lecture and the oral class, you have the chance to listen to the same thing ten times over if you want to. Where the lecturer and other students can be annoyed at too many requests for repetition, machines never tire.

Conversation classes

During the talking time of your course you have a different kind of challenge. Instead of listening and taking things down you are expected to listen and take part. The two are closely linked. Your listening develops as you find yourself responding and sometimes finding out, directly or indirectly, that you have misheard. Some students referred to extra, voluntary conversation classes. They are a great way to increase your chances to listen actively.

Out-of-class opportunities

Beyond the timetabled programme, here are some more listening opportunities.

Foreign-language films and videos in the audio-visual library

Watching movies can be a relatively relaxed way of learning by listening. You learn to improve your listening in quite specific ways. Take them home for extra practice. Successful students mention the importance of repetition. Understanding comes gradually, increasing the more you listen, although it is worth noting that listening for hours to sounds you don't understand at all won't do much for your language learning.

Conversations on cassette-tape

Some conversations designed for language practice will also be available in other forms, such as audio-cassette, video-cassette and compact disk. Particularly at the early stages of language learning these small chunks of language are useful. They may even have an accompanying textbook so that you can look at the script as you follow the sound. Many people who have learned mainly through the printed word find it useful to make this connection.

The foreign-language play

This has been mentioned already as good for listening and for other aspects of language development. If you are an actor in a play you will be having plenty of practice but even if you are not, why not volunteer for one of the other roles that involve listening as you attend rehearsals: stage hand, costuming and so on? Even the ticket sellers can slip in after the first few minutes.

Beyond the course

Going a step further than what is provided within your institution, students report further ideas.

attending gatherings where the language was spoken

Find out what these could include in your area. Are there groups of expatriates who enjoy welcoming language students? How about a film club?

listening to native speakers

When individual native speakers become tired of providing language for you to listen to then let technology take over. Students report making full use of commercially available resources, showing considerable ingenuity in making chances to listen to native speakers. Foreign radio programmes are probably the most easily accessible. Students also refer to karaoke and other forms of music.

For those whose finances allow it or who can find employment, there is always

visiting countries where the language was spoken

Some of these visits include home stays, which are recommended as a way of being totally immersed in the language for as long as you stay in the house. Travelling to the country with other English-speaking people is comfortable but you need to be more disciplined about which language you use when and where.

Listen to friends

Friends who are learning the language can be called upon, sometimes in an arrangement that pins down a particular time of the week to meet.

Fellow students can be more tolerant of long pauses and re-phrasing than native speakers are. More than one student *asked friends fluent in the language to speak to me in it*. There is a difference though in the quality of the input. One student comments that people should try to have *'As much contact with true French accents* [as possible. It is] *much better as it can be a shock.'*

Listen to yourself

Some students find that it helps to listen to themselves. One of them reads aloud onto tape and then listens to her voice, following the text at the same time.

8.3 TYPES OF LISTENING

Whatever type of listening you organise for yourself, there are two main purposes for listening as part of your foreign-language class. One is the same reason as you have in any language – because you want to hear what is being said; the other is in order to focus mainly on the language used. The more you listen to messages where the meaning is important to you, the better. Not only will you want to hear more, but you will also be absorbing more language with little effort.

The other reason is that listening helps your language learning. In the end these two purposes must come together, as this language student expresses it.

> I just listened to people speak. It took a long time to make sense of what appeared to be small foreign units of sound that meant nothing. Slowly nouns, verbs and adjectives became familiar and then finally the grammar fell in around them to make sensible units.

Listening for content

In this case you are more interested in the message than the language, although without your realising it your listening skills will be improving at the same time. Listening for content includes deciding what the purpose of the text is. Is the speaker trying mainly to entertain, to persuade, to inform, to confess or simply to make social contact? Establishing this at the start will help you make better sense of the whole thing.

As you listen to the content the same process will be happening as when you read. You will be making connections between what you know already and the new information you hear.

Listening for language points

We turn now to ways of listening in order to focus mainly on language points. In this case you could choose to listen to more complicated language than you are actually able to produce yourself, as a way of training yourself to fill in the gaps in your understanding. The advice from some students about listening to tapes even on boring topics simply in order to learn more seems harsh. Ideally of course you will find material that has at least some interest for you.

Here are some ways of making your listening an active process.

Listen for new features

General listening is one thing but you can also follow one student's advice to be specific in your listening.

> If one wants to learn how to speak naturally, I think one has to listen carefully to native-speaker speech. I think learners should pick some aspect of language they are interested in or that they think they are weak in, and listen (or read) for those items in conversations/TVprogrammes/articles etc. For example, in Japanese the subtleties of expression are not only made through tone of voice etc., but through adverbs (more so than in English). I have noticed that non-native speakers of Japanese tend not to be able to use these 'expressive adverbs' particularly well. The ones who can are generally regarded as the most 'fluent'. While I was in Japan last year I made the effort to listen for those 'expressive adverbs' in conversation and have tried to use them more when I speak in Japanese. Through my mistakes I am learning how to use them properly, and hopefully becoming more native-like.

Like this student, you could choose to listen for particular features of the spoken language such as the intonation patterns, particularly when there are big differences with your own language. You could listen for pace. Is the other language generally spoken faster, more slowly or at the same pace as English? Of course there are individual differences but you will probably also notice some patterns. Here are some questions to direct your thinking about features of the new language.

1.   Are there any pairs of sounds that are hard for you to differentiate?
Hearing differences between several tones has to happen before you can make the differences yourself.

2.   Listen for new phrases, idioms and grammatical structures
How do people put groups of words together? Are they the same patterns as in the written language? Can you hear any chunks of language which are made up of individual words with meanings of their own but which are often heard as a unit with a special meaning? Examples of these in English are:

> *would you mind*
> *on the other hand*
> *taking into account*

Of course, things can sometimes sound new because you haven't made the connection with the written form you already know. Another problem is when people fail to recognise proper names and are going to the dictionary to look up the word '*Gwangchou*' (an area of China), for example.

Listen for familiar words in new contexts

When you are listening to, say, a movie, sometimes you can make yourself notice particular words and phrases that you have started to learn already. Notice how they are used. Do they seem to be used mainly in formal contexts or informal? Are they words used more by children than by adults? Listen too for words that are familiar because they are international words or borrowed words. Many commercial products have the same name all over the world (Pepsi, Levis) although the actual pronunciation may be different. If your language and the new one have a lot of words in common then you have a slightly easier task, once you have worked out the pronunciation.

Note features you are ready to use yourself

Listen for the elements of the new language that you find yourself ready to use. Are you tired of saying everything in the same few verb tenses? If so, listen for some of the more complicated tenses and write down examples as you listen. Are you using the same few phrases for the same purposes all the time? Start to notice how speakers introduce their digressions ('By the way . . .'), their disagreements ('Fine but . . .') and their endings to conversations ('Well, it's been good chatting . . .'). In other words, compare the language you are currently using with the language that other people use, particularly native speakers.

Watch body language

When you are listening face to face or to a video, some of the meaning comes from the speakers' facial expressions and body movements. Body language is influenced by tradition and by the individuality of a particular speaker. Some language speakers make more use of these than others but even in languages where the speakers make little use of arm and hand gestures there will be some clues.

Summary

What happens as you listen as part of language learning is that not only your listening ability but other aspects of your language learning improve too. As one student puts it:

> As I got quicker at speaking German, my understanding of others speaking it improved.

Active listening to conversations

In the first part of this chapter we looked at how listening can move from being passive to being interactive (see Figure 8.1). Let us consider now some ways of taking your active listening a step further in particular situations. One of the most active types of listening is taking part in a conversation, especially if there are only two of you talking. As well as being ready with an answer, you need to have a number of other strategies ready in case you don't understand what is being said. Here are some that good listeners report.

Act as if you understand

This may sound like strange advice. What is the point of pretending you understand if you don't? One reason is that often what you have failed to understand will become clear as the conversation continues. If the speaker seems to be asking for agreement or disagreement, some sort of meaningful murmur from you may encourage him to keep going, elaborating the original point in a way that will help you understand it. This strategy also stops you from spending too much time when you don't understand. It is a technique that little children use in their own language. They laugh at the jokes of their older brothers and sisters even when they can't see the point. The result is that they get included in the ongoing conversation. Native speakers will go on talking if they think you are following.

Indicate non-understanding

Here is the opposite advice. When you realise that it is crucial to the conversation that you understand some detail, ask. There are many ways of asking. The most obvious is to say the equivalent of 'I beg your pardon?' or 'Could you say that again please?' This usually leads to a repetition of the earlier message, which may or may not be helpful. Many native speakers of a language have limited experience of speaking with a language learner. They have only two tactics. They say it again or they shout it, neither of which helps unless you also have a hearing problem. Often what you need is not a repeat but a re-wording ('What's another word for . . . ?'). Help get yourself and the other person out of this trap by asking questions like 'Such as?' or by looking puzzled.

A strategy that is less helpful is asking the other person to slow down. Some people don't really know how to speak slowly. Instead, they speak artificially. The most useful kind of slowness is when people leave pauses between their sentences so that you have time to absorb the message.

It is helpful if you can be precise about what you don't know.

> When talking to a native speaker I would try to home in on the word I didn't know and ask for clarification.

If you are not sure which of two words has been said, then indicate that ('Did you say . . . or . . . ?'). This question shows that you are listening and following most of the message but have been tripped up by one word only. Asking people the meaning of words they have used is something we are doing all the time in our own language too, so it doesn't really slow down a conversation.

Sometimes you need more than the sound of a word in order to understand.

I ask the spelling of words. I need to see it written down often to understand the pronunciation.

Often you may switch between this kind of concentrated listening for
form and the more general listening for meaning, as another student
reports.

I tried 'opening' my ears to get the general meaning and avoid getting stuck
on a particular word.

Use your common sense

Failing all else, use your common sense or, to put it more technically,
use all the clues you can from the surrounding context. If someone asks
you to come to dinner at a time that sounds unusual for the part of the
world where you are at that moment, the chances are that you have
misheard and need to say so immediately, before you miss out on your
meal.

Listening practice in pairs and small groups

Many students speak about having conversations with one another. As
well as general conversations, you can organise listening 'games' which
don't take much preparation. Here are a few ideas:

Give map instructions
Have a map open in front of you while your friend gives you instructions
for finding the way from one point to another. Pointing is not allowed.

Describe a picture
Both of you look at the same picture. One starts describing the picture,
deliberately adding some extra details. As soon as the other hears some
wrong information he or she corrects the information and carries on the
description. The idea is to see how long you can keep going before being
stopped. You can do this even at a beginner's level. At a more advanced
level you need to include also strategies for getting the other person to
repeat, or to explain ambiguities.

Build on the last comment
Practise drawing out a conversation by making every remark join in
some way to the previous one. Time yourselves. See if you can carry on
a longer and longer conversation each week.

Dictate a picture
Sketch a quick picture on your own piece of paper and then dictate it to the other person. This can work well with the flags of various countries.

Listening by yourself

Some of the listening that students report doing is quite solitary. They sit in the computer or language laboratory or they take home tapes. The following suggestions are for making the most of listening alone.

Listen first, write later

Some time after you have listened to a tape with factual information (a few hours later or even the next day), try writing out some of the information you have heard. This could be in note form or in sentences. Then listen again to the tape and see how much you have remembered. This will tell you something about the depth of listening you are doing. Are you storing the new ideas in your memory for later recall?

Think about the meaning

This suggestion is a development of an earlier one. Separate the times when you listen for meaning and those when you listen for language points. When you are attending to the meaning you will be absorbing the language as well but in a slightly more relaxed way. You could make yourself listen for something particular. For instance, if you are listening to a news broadcast through satellite two or three times a week, before you start, try to recall some of the news items you heard last time and pose some questions you expect to hear answered this time. Supposing the last news you heard was about a terrorist attack somewhere. Then you could listen today for this information:

Do they know who did it and why?
Has anyone been caught?
Is this linked with any other recent attacks?
What are national or world leaders saying about it?
Are steps being taken to prevent further attacks?
What is happening to the survivors?

Make inferences

When we listen to spoken language we are listening at many levels. The most obvious level is the actual facts being given: who did what, when and where. However, we are also listening for deeper meaning. The further you advance with your language learning the better you will be able to make inferences from your reading. Of course, this also depends on having a good background knowledge of the place and times being written about. If you read, 'She threw open her suitcase and started to fling in some clothing for her January holiday,' you would need to know whether the character was in Sydney or London in order to picture the sort of clothes being flung in.

Turn down the sound

If you are watching a video with plenty of dialogue, try listening once and then turning down the sound the second time. Then try saying the words along with the speakers. Finally, listen once more to see how close your meaning is.

Listen to a variety of voices

From time to time assess the listening you are doing to see whether you are finding a variety of models. Here are some ranges to think about:

adults', children's, men's and women's voices,
formal and informal language,
uninterrupted talk, and interaction between several people,
talk at different speeds,
different accents.

Listen and . . . ?

Many kinds of listening require a response. Table 8.1 shows three contexts for listening and the kind of response you could make.

The final point to keep in mind is that eventually you will want to listen in your new language for all the reasons that you listen in your first. Everything you do as practice can lead sooner or later to enjoyable and varied listening.

TABLE 8.1 CONTEXTS AND RESPONSES FOR LISTENING

Context	Response
Lectures	note taking, remembering
Conversations	taking part
Tape-recordings	give yourself a dictation, focus on one aspect of the language

8.4 PRACTICAL IDEAS FOR LISTENING

Make up a quiz

Here is an idea for beginners in a language. Make up general knowledge questions:

Who is the president of——?
Which year did——?
What country has——?

Use the answerphone

Arrange for a group of students to leave answerphone messages for one another.

Listening to the news

1. Tape the foreign-language broadcast each day (or access the version that is already available in your multi-media centre). Compare it with the English-language version of the international news from your newspaper, TV or radio.
2. As you listen to the news, copy down phrases that are repeated and tick the number of times you hear them. Start adding the most frequent phrases to your vocabulary collection. They are likely to be even more up-to-date than your dictionary.
3. Have the same key questions to answer for each news broadcast.

Who are the key people involved?
Where are they?
What is happening?
Why are these events happening?
When did the events take place?
How do the events affect other people?

Assess your listening strategies

Take notes as you listen to a piece of connected language (a lecture, talk, broadcast). Afterwards look critically at your notes. How do they compare with your note-taking in English? Are you able to get the main point of the talk or just a few details? Can you distinguish between new points and illustrations of the last point? Keep working at your note-taking skills.

Have regular video evenings

Ask friends round to watch a video from your foreign-language video library. At the end, insist on a foreign-language-only discussion of what you have seen. A supply of food helps to lure people along in the first place and to keep them there for the discussion.

9

Speaking Fluently

There are many stages along the way to being a fluent speaker of a new language. Some learners like to plunge into conversations, improving the finer points of pronunciation and expression as they go. Others prefer to work hard at the right pronunciation, intonation and stress from the start so that they are well prepared when they start talking. Whatever your general approach, the main advice in this chapter is that people learn to speak by speaking, so make the opportunities and start.

If you are an outgoing, talkative person in your own language, then you probably won't need persuading to start talking. On the other hand, if you tend to be a better listener than talker, then this chapter has suggestions for improving the amount and quality of your speaking. First, here is some information about how people learn to speak in a new language.

9.1 The process of learning to speak

In learning to speak, you need to attend to the same aspects of language that apply to listening, reading and writing. You need to:

1. Pronounce the words and sentences in ways that other people can understand (the form of the language).
2. Observe the social rules of speaking.

3. Know a variety of ways of linking your ideas, including fitting them to what others are saying.
4. Overcome problems in communicating in a language you are still learning.

Eventually, as with listening, you are going to need to speak in a range of contexts, some more difficult than others such as:

on the telephone / face to face,
with friends / with strangers,
on familiar topics / on topics introduced by others,
about work / about social and personal matters.

The form of the language

Getting the language 'right' used to be the main thrust of language learning. Now people realise that a few slips in pronunciation don't necessarily destroy meaning, but pronunciation does hinder communication if speakers have the wrong stress, rhythm, pitch, and intonation to the point where they are incomprehensible to others. It doesn't hinder communication if the speaker simply has a slightly different pronunciation from native speakers. After all, in most languages there is a huge range of accents amongst native speakers themselves.

The way a person speaks (their accent) has been described as the most individual aspect of their use of language. It says something about the part of the country they come from, the sort of family they live with and other more personal traits. You can get quite emotional responses when people criticise one another's accents. The same can be true of pronouncing a foreign language. Some learners are looking forward to the day when people mistake them for native speakers. For most people this is not going to happen for a long time, if ever, but that shouldn't matter. Even among the speakers of one language there are many, many different ways of speaking and a range of accents that people can understand.

The main point about pronunciation is that although you work hard at remembering how to make the sounds exactly like a model, what really counts is being understood. However, as many language learners know, pronunciation, even more than finding words and structures, is something that can hold up speaking if a person keeps stopping in mid-sentence to get the exact sound right. That's the fastest way to lose an audience.

Remembering how to pronounce seems to be a process of hearing good models many times, repeating the sounds in context both for practice and in real conversations, and also monitoring your pronunciation. Gradually, as we shall see in the chapter on speaking, your pronunciation comes closer and closer to the model you are listening to.

The sounds of the language need to be practised through many kinds of talking, rather than through hours of repeating tricky sound combinations. Some concentrated practice certainly helps, including the many electronic support systems available, particularly at the beginners' stage. For example, one computer-based series of lessons has visual representations of Chinese tones. Using these for short periods of time can make a difference eventually but getting pronunciation right seems to be a continuing process of adjusting and readjusting the categories of what learners hear and what they can produce.

Think about whether you are at the 'correctness' or 'accuracy' end of the continuum when it comes to your approach to speaking. Does either of these students sounds like you? They are both very conscious of the form of the language they are using.

> I like speaking slowly and clearly, thinking before speaking about the word order and agreement.

> When I use German in everyday conversations with English speakers I think what I'll say in German first.

Other students approach their speaking in the same spontaneous way as they would in their first language. In your own language, of course, you can speak both accurately and fluently. Try asking yourself whether you need to be paying more attention to correctness or to fluency in your learning.

Overcoming pronunciation problems

What are some of the difficulties in pronouncing a new language? There is more to it than just making the sounds.

Isolating difficulties

You may break the problem down into segments of problems, such as a particular sound, but that sound must then be placed in a bigger group. For example, you may find it difficult to pronounce a group of sounds at the end of a word. These must be put into longer utterances for the purpose of practice. You will know already which sounds in your language do not exist in the new one and these are not a problem. It's the other way round that is difficult: new sounds and new combinations of sounds.

Overcoming feelings

Another problem has to do with people's feelings. Some language learners feel really odd at first when speaking another language. That may be because the new language has sounds that make them feel childish. Some say, for instance, that making the Spanish /th/ sound where English would have /s/ makes them feel like babies.

Using the correct word stress

Then there is the question of where to put the emphasis within words. In some languages this is crucial to meaning and in other languages it may make the difference between being and not being understood. In languages such as Spanish and Italian, words look very familiar because, like their English equivalents, they have come from Latin, and yet the stress seems to fall in a different part of the word. After a while, if you are a good listener, these new stress patterns will become natural and you will see that within the new language they have a pattern of their own. This means that you do not have to learn how to say each new word separately.

Using intonation to express meaning

Intonation is another part of speaking in a way that others can understand you. Within an utterance people's voices go up and down in patterns that express basic meaning or let you know the speaker's feelings. Although some books indicate intonation patterns by using symbols, most people seem to find that listening and imitating are the most effective ways of learning. Search out a range of models for your speaking. One student had a good suggestion:

> I've started listening to the [community] radio station for Chinese and Japanese and taping it. Then I speak with native speakers.

Find out whether there are accessible radio broadcasts on local-community language stations. They will have the advantage of talking about familiar events.

Learning the social rules

Another aspect of speaking to be mastered is the social rules of the language. Unlike writing, when you speak your audience is either right there with you or at the end of a telephone waiting for you to carry on. In Chapter 14 you'll read some aspects of cross-cultural communication and how they can affect good speaking and listening. Here, in brief, are the sorts of questions you will be finding answers to as you converse with native speakers of the language:

Who has status in this speech community?
    e.g., Should I speak differently to my friends' parents or to other older people?
What difference does status make when speaking?
    e.g., Should I wait for the other person to speak first?
When are different uses of language appropriate?
    e.g., Is complaining out of place in some contexts?
How much should I express my own opinions?
    e.g., Are opinions something to share only with friends?

This is one area of speaking where practising with your fellow students is not much help because you will all be following the same rules of politeness and appropriateness.

Making links between ideas

In conversation you need to know how to move from one idea and one speaker to the next. That includes joining your own ideas in ways that go beyond 'and . . . and . . . and' as well as getting a turn while others are speaking. This last point is important. Language learners often feel they are back to childhood, with everyone talking above their heads and no way of getting a turn. Part of the problem is, of course, a listening problem rather than a speaking problem. It is easy to have a general sense of a conversation but when you add something it is embarrassing to notice that everyone is surprised to hear what you have said, as if it didn't belong there. When people say, 'You're off the track,' or 'What's that got to do with it?' you know there's a problem, but at least you can repair it.

Linking ideas means being able to continue a topic smoothly so that you don't sound abrupt. The links are often quite different in writing and in speech. Although nobody today would recommend memorising pages of language, learning by heart some formulas for particular occasions to keep the conversation flowing can be useful. Examples of fixed phrases in English include.

By the way, sorry about that, all things considered, could you possibly . . . ?

Overcoming communication problems

Finally, speaking involves verbal and non-verbal strategies to compensate for breakdowns in communication (such as forgetting a word or how to pronounce it) and to enhance the effectiveness of your own communication (as in deliberately slowing down or changing tone for effect).

One solution when you forget the right word is to choose a paraphrase instead of the ideal word ('the place where you get food' instead of 'the cafeteria'), a strategy we use in our first language. Try to learn many general words like 'person', 'place', 'thing' to describe what you mean even when the exact word is missing. Sometimes a quick action fills the gap, particularly if you don't mind looking a bit theatrical. One person in a Japanese supermarket forgot the word for chicken and had to resort to making the right sounds as she flapped her arms to get her meaning across. Asking people to help is another useful strategy ('What do you call the things that . . . ?'). That way you have a chance of remembering the word next time.

How does speaking help general language development?

Speaking helps with your writing, reading and listening. It turns out that speaking (and of course writing, as we'll see in Chapter 13) is important for the whole learning process. It helps your fluency and it also helps your accuracy.

Speaking makes you a more fluent language user

As you talk you become more skilled at all the strategies for overcoming problems in communication. You also become less focused on the way you are talking ('Is my pronunciation funny?') than on what you want to say, because the other person is waiting. This is not the same as saying

that 'practice makes perfect'. It is certainly possible to speak fluently
and inaccurately for a long time.

Speaking is a chance to notice the gaps

When learners are speaking (either out loud or, as some report, under
their breath) they often notice a gap between what they want to say and
what they can say. They notice what they *don't* know, or know only
partially. The smart student can then do something about those gaps
which give you a hint about what areas of language you need to spend
more time on.

Speaking is a chance to test hypotheses

A third purpose for speaking is to test your hypotheses about language.
A hypothesis is a 'rule' you are starting to formulate, such as the fact
that the answer to A can be B, C or D, or that people when they first
meet seem to say such and such.

Mistakes in particular bring feedback, which leads you to modify
your understanding and to make adjustments as you go on talking. Of
course this is not happening all the time. Sometimes you are so absorbed
in your topic that you don't think much about the language. Some
learners reflect on the form of the language, while still concentrating
on getting meaning across. A couple of language learners explain that
while they are speaking they become aware of the fact that some forms
are not 'correct' and amend them.

Learn from the language of others

This point really relates to listening except that speaking of course
creates the opportunities for more listening. One thing is certain. If you
want to be able to speak in a range of contexts, as listed at the start of
the chapter, you need to hear a range of models. As we have seen, this
is now possible through advances in technology for computer programs,
but even with only a radio, many students have achieved remarkable
clarity in their pronunciation of a new language.

9.2 MAKING OPPORTUNITIES TO SPEAK

Successful students' suggestions for practice vary between genuine communication and 'artificial' things you can do. As a language student you

have some ready-made contexts for speaking, such as tutorials, where the whole purpose is to become better speakers and listeners. You can also create opportunities to speak with other language students or with people you know who have learned the language already. Then there is the ultimate test of your language learning – using it with native speakers. In between these stages there is always talking to yourself, which many students said was an important part of language learning. We'll look at how you can use each of these chances to the maximum.

One way of planning your speaking is to think of all the contexts in which you would like to speak eventually and make sure that you have practice in all of them. Here are a few:

> asking for information from strangers,
> exchanging ideas with friends,
> giving short talks,
> joining in casual conversations.

Joining in language tutorials

Are you one of the people who sit in language tutorials wishing they could have a turn or are you one of those who dread being asked to speak? This section has some practical advice on the sort of questions you can ask or comments you can make to get a turn. Try one new idea each day.

Ask information questions
This is the simplest type of question you can ask the teacher but at least it gets you a turn, for example, 'Could you give us some ideas for translating the phrase . . . in this passage?'

State your opinion
In the context of discussing literature, be ready to give your opinion. This does not have to involve saying something momentous about a whole novel, for example, 'The passage that seemed to be most unusual/ effective was . . .'

Make connections with other reading
If you do even minimal preparation before the tutorial you should be able to make a connection between today's reading and yesterday's, for example, 'That passage reminded me of . . .'

Report your reading predictions
Talk about the thoughts you had while you were reading, don't wait until you have finished, for example, 'When I reached this point in the story I thought . . .'

Make inferences
As with listening, there is far more to reading than the surface meaning. Try to draw inferences from the text, for example, 'She doesn't actually say this but it seems . . .'

Make generalisations
When you have read more than one piece by the same author or from the same period you are ready to make some generalisations, even if you put them in the form of a question, for example, 'Judging by the three poems we've read so far, it seems that this writer tends to . . .'

Justify your viewpoints
Sometimes the tutor or lecturer will ask you to justify your statement in a discussion. Some people get very nervous about this and leave it all to the most confident students. Don't be overwhelmed by those who talk fastest and loudest. Your quiet contribution will be just as important, for example, 'In my opinion . . .' or 'This is the effect it had on me . . .'

Other ideas

Here is a summary of other ways of joining in the class discussion.

Adding information to someone else's points,
Agreeing or disagreeing,
Asking for clarification,
Giving examples (from other reading, your own experience or that of other people),
Presenting both sides of an argument,
Suggesting an untested hypothesis.

Speaking with other language learners

The key here is to find people with the same goal as yourself – to speak in the new language, at whatever level you have reached. One student mentions the importance of regular arrangements. 'I met with two friends for Spanish conversation once a week.' Students at the same level as yourself can be useful allies. On the other hand, if you imitate the student who said, 'Try to speak with people who have a higher level of the language than you,' then you are halfway towards being able to communicate with native speakers. If you want to challenge yourself, this could be a good approach.

Discussions

There are many ways of organising the time you spend talking. One is to run it as a loose discussion time with people taking turns to nominate topics and to keep the conversation going. Here are some suggestions for topics you are already familiar with, so that your efforts don't have to go into thinking of what to say:

> memories of your childhood,
> highlights of your extra-curricular reading,
> your plans for when you have finished studying,
> ideas for earning extra money as a student,
> recent movies,
> experiences of travelling,
> unusual sights from the past week,
> places you would like to visit.

Notice that some of these topics force you to use particular grammatical structures such as the past, the future or the conditional.

Language games and activities

Alternatively you could look at some of the books of communication activities that have been written for language learners. It doesn't really matter what language the book refers to; the type of activity is what counts. These force you to exchange ideas by overcoming communication problems. For example, there are activities where one of you has information that the other needs and you take turns at giving and asking for the information needed. Here are some more ideas:

1. Guessing games such as Twenty Questions.
2. Role-playing familiar situations.
3. Decision making. (What would you take if you had only a few minutes to rescue your possessions from a burning house?)

4. Card games. (If you can bear to revisit your childhood, games like Happy Families can easily be played by language beginners because they give plenty of practice in repeating simple constructions.)

These are just a few of dozens of ideas you can find in books for language students.

Talking to yourself

There are a number of reasons why talking to yourself helps prepare you for talking with others. You don't have to worry about the effect you are having and you can take as much time as you want to. You can also say the same thing several times without being thought strange. One student who found that talking to himself helped build up his confidence, described his progress in French like this:

> I was a listener more than a speaker but when I did eventually put an effort into my speaking, my knowledge of the written code and grammars was far beyond my speaking ability which helped immensely to become reasonably proficient in the language. Confidence was the biggest thing to overcome, or should I say lack of it. I could hear my English accent when I spoke French, and I hated it. So I would go around repeating sentences and colloquial sayings over and over, either in my mind or out loud. This helped me master the strange vowel and consonant sounds that French has and improved my confidence, which seemed to be directly correlated to my progress.

Here are some other variations on the theme of talking to yourself.

Reading out loud with only yourself as an audience was a favourite. Many students suggest this:

> Say examples and texts out loud.

Even reading the textbook out loud was mentioned as a way of giving confidence in speaking and letting the patterns of the language 'sound in your head'. In your own language you know when you have made a slip of the tongue because it sounds wrong. This knowledge takes longer with a new language.

Having something to start the speaking is a help. One student sat with a set of photographs and used them as a source of ideas. Another tried translating.

> I used to and still do read something in English and figure out how I would
> say it in French.

Even silent speaking is useful. One student liked

> saying phrases aloud and in my head in the everyday situations in which
> they fitted, practising the language by making myself think in it and speak it
> to myself.

If you record yourself speaking and then listen, you may be able to
monitor your own progress and decide on what aspects of your language
you want to work at. Here are a few of the problems people have with
pronouncing a new language. You could listen for them when you
replay the tape.

> Giving the wrong length to vowels.
> Making or not making liaisons between words.
> Stressing the wrong syllable.
> Putting in the pauses in odd places.

Time is a worry to many students. 'That's a great idea', they say, 'but
I'm too busy doing assignments.' Here's how one student found the
time.

> Whenever I had some 'free mental time' e.g. on the bus, I would run little
> conversations in my head in French or Italian, trying to get as close as I
> could to what I wanted to say.

Conversations with native speakers

Students emphasise the importance of using the new language naturally.

> Try saying things in those languages in normal life to become fluent.

Finding people to talk with who have the patience to listen, especially when you are at the early stages, can be a challenge. Understandably people can start giving a wide berth to students whose need to talk
is greater than their actual message.

I talked in French or Italian to anyone who wouldn't get angry at me for babbling away.

However, it's worth persisting. As one student put it:

I recommend speaking with Chinese people and more speaking with Chinese people.

We have already mentioned the idea of conversational exchange partners, but not all conversations with native speakers are face to face. When telephone costs are not prohibitive you can try setting up the spoken equivalent of correspondence, and if e-mail can be counted as halfway to talking, then that is another cheap and easily accessible option.

Whoever you choose to speak with, do it regularly and often. One student who had been given an A in Latin but a B + in French came up with her own reason for the difference. 'I don't practise speaking enough.' Assuming you want to speak and you have found some native speakers who are willing to talk, what is there to say? In this next section there are suggestions for taking part in genuine exchanges with native speakers.

9.3   What do I say?

We'll look now at four types of conversation you might have with native speakers.

Conversations with friends

Whereas in speaking a different language with other English speakers you can follow the same conversational rules as you do in your own language, with native speakers of the other language you have to follow their rules. (See the section on 'Cross-cultural Communication' in Chapter 14.) Start to imitate what you have noticed about the other people's stages of conversation.

I   The opening

How long do they spend on small talk before getting to the point? In some cultures there will be very little, perhaps none, whereas in others it seems to take ages to get to the point.

What sort of things do they talk about at the beginning of a conversation? Are there more general comments (the weather, the state of the nation) or more personal comments (one another's clothes and lives). Do people tend to start with observations or questions?

2 The heart of the conversation

What sort of topics interest people of your own age in the other culture? Do they enjoy discussing the news of the day, including international events, or do they prefer more philosophical and abstract discussions about life in general?

3 Ending the conversation

How many moves are there before a conversation ends? How do you signal that it's time to go? Are the exchanges fairly predictable or do people tend to say original things right at the last minute?

Service exchanges

Service exchanges may be all the real-life exchanges you have a chance to use if you visit a country where the language is spoken. They include exchanges with hairdressers, waiters and waitresses, airline booking staff, shopkeepers and so on. In some of these places the exchanges are more predictable than in others and you can prepare yourself for them. If you are going to a booking office, for example, or to a doctor's reception room to make an appointment, then it is easier to predict what will happen. There are only so many questions that you can expect to be asked. It's a question of being ready with the appropriate answers. This is the sort of exchange you can practise with your friends beforehand. Just remember, though, that the person in the office has not read your language textbook. You need to be ready for the exchange to take a different turn.

Other exchanges are less ritualistic, and when you are in public places you could start to notice what others say as well as concentrating on your own encounter. Standing in a queue waiting for service is a legitimate time for eavesdropping. People seem to manage to eavesdrop too on restaurant encounters, especially when the tables are close together.

Encounters with strangers

When you are travelling you can often have chances to practise your language. If you are waiting in an airport lounge or travelling in a long-distance bus you can find yourself enjoying conversations that add to your understanding of the other culture. You may even be able to ask strangers about aspects of language use that have been bothering you ('Why do people say . . . sometimes and . . . at other times?'). You will find, though, that many people cannot answer questions about their own language. They know how to use it but they haven't learned to analyse it.

Revealing that you know something about the country's history can lead to interesting conversations. A word of caution here. It is easy to start talking about the more sensational aspects of countries' histories without thinking that you could be on dangerous ground. Let the other person raise the topic of lost battles and political scandals if they want to.

The other person will have questions too. When travelling you can find yourself slipping into the role of expert spokesperson on many aspects of your country's culture. Be ready to talk about anything from current fashions in clothes and music to the political system as it has developed this century.

Telling jokes

This is one of the hardest things to do in another language, as illustrated by the story of an interpreter at an international conference. He didn't see how he could translate a joke that had been made in the middle of a speech, so he said, 'The delegate from . . . has just said something that is very funny in his own language. I suggest you all laugh.'

However, if everyone else is telling jokes, why not have a try? If your command of the language is good enough you may even be able to adapt some details to suit the local context. In fact, apart from puns, it is not the language aspect that makes it difficult to tell jokes in another language; you can get by with quite simple language. It's knowing what people will find funny as opposed to pointless or distasteful.

You could take some current jokes in English and try to retell them in the foreign language. Note that of course this doesn't necessarily make them funny to native speakers of the other language but it could entertain your fellow students.

9.4 PRACTICAL IDEAS FOR SPEAKING

Babysitting

If you have the chance to mind young children who speak the language you are learning, there will be plenty of chances to speak. There is less embarrassment as you play games or even read to them in their own language from books in their home.

Give dictations

Try giving a dictation to other students. They will soon tell you if you are not speaking clearly.

Spot the difference

This is a good one for beginners. Collect some of those 'spot the difference' pictures that appear in the children's pages of magazines. Then take turns at telling each other the differences. You can do this with even minimal language. Remember to avoid pointing and using words like 'this one' and 'here'.

Polite interruptions

This can work with two or more people. Decide on a topic and then appoint a starter. To have a turn at speaking the others have to interrupt in some way that makes a clear link with what has just been said. For example:

> That reminds me . . .
> Oh yes and another example is . . .
> Does that mean you think . . .

Tell stories

This is a version of a children's game. A group of you takes turns to tell the next sentence in a story. Use your imaginations. If nobody understands what you have said you have to try again. You can make up rules such as being allowed to use one English word per sentence.

Practise your class presentations

Some people get very nervous about having to speak in front of a whole class. If you are one of these, take time beforehand to present your talk to a friend and vice versa. Give each other feedback on aspects of the delivery, including speed and making eye contact.

Conclusion

The answers to our questionnaire show that language students are very innovative in their ideas for practising speaking. Try exchanging suggestions with your fellow students for overcoming problems and for giving yourselves more practise in speaking.

10

LEARNING GRAMMAR

> *The word 'grammar' has unpleasant connotations for many people. For some it means reciting rules and then trying to apply them at the right time. For others it means everything about the structure of the new language that is different from the language they speak already. This chapter builds on the information in Chapter 2 about knowing and describing a language, by showing not what you need to learn but how you can learn it.*

Speaking broadly, there are two ways people find out the grammar of a new language. One is to learn the rules (either through being told them or through reading them) and the other is to discover them. Many people learn through both approaches at the same time. Let's look at what is involved in each process.

10.1 PROCESSES OF LEARNING GRAMMAR

Formal learning

Learning the rules formally and then trying to apply them in various situations requires either a teacher or a book. Your teacher/lecturer may combine formal and informal learning by asking you to try and discover the rules for yourself before he or she puts the rule into words. You can actually ask yourself the sort of questions teachers ask about a reading passage. Here are some examples.

1. *What is the main idea here?*
   It's no good trying to work out a rule if you don't know what the whole passage is about.

2. *How does the arrangement of the words make this meaning clear?*
   For example, in some languages the words and phrases can be put in
   different orders to give emphasis to part of the message.

3. *What is special about the way the words are put together here?*
   Compare this way of saying things with the effect if you changed
   around one or two words or phrases.

4. *Are there any similar examples in the rest of the text?*
   Try to see a pattern in the structure. Does it seem to be used for a
   particular effect such as expressing surprise, emphasising a detail, or
   making a comparison?

5. *What would happen if we changed some of the words?*
   How much of the meaning is in the individual words and how much
   in the way they are put together?

After you have answered all these questions, it's time to try and formulate a rule. You could express the rule in terms of the way the words are
put together ('I can see how those word endings are formed') or the
meaning it conveys ('So that's how they say sorry'). Finally you could go
to a grammar reference book to check your understanding or you could
ask questions at the next tutorial.

Why, you may ask, would I waste all that time asking myself
questions when I could go straight to the final step of asking or looking
it up? The reason has to do with the learning process, including
memory, as mentioned in Chapter 4. Something you are told or that you
read once stays in your memory for less time than something you have
worked out for yourself. That is because spending more energy on
understanding information seems to embed it in the mind more deeply.

A final note on formal grammar learning. Students say that if they
have already learned the grammar of their own language in a formal
way, then it is easier to learn the grammar of the new one in the same
way. Those who haven't, say that learning the grammar of a foreign
language has helped them look at their own language in a new way. The
experience of one such learner goes like this.

Not having been taught any English grammar at school I had to go back to
the basics and learn noun, verb, adjective, adverb etc. After I had mastered the basic structure, the more difficult French grammar became less
daunting and even appeared logical.

Choosing a grammar reference book

Your university or school textbook will have grammar explanations all the way through it. Still, many students like to choose their own grammar reference book that sees them through two or three years. If you are one of those people, it's worth taking time to choose a book that suits you and the way you like to study from the many available for the language you are learning. It's just a question of searching until you find the right one. One student reported buying more than one extra grammar book to help with his Spanish studies. Another describes what he wants in a grammar book.

> I want the grammar divided up into easy chunks. One page at a time is good. They should explain the point and then give you an exercise to see if you've got it. The best book has the answers in the back. That's very important. I have to use it without a teacher. They should give you practical examples you can go out and use right away. When you come to look up the index you need to find easy words there. Some of the words in the index I can't understand. All I want is one book for all the grammar points I need to know, not three different levels. Pictures and cartoons are quite good at the beginning stages but they have to be something I can get the point of, like international things, not too subtle. Sometimes the joke is funny to the speakers of that language but not to me. In a grammar book I just want grammar, not cultural things.

There are many types of grammar book available now. For example, there are academic grammars for advanced language learners, including native speakers, teachers' grammars which, again, some advanced students like to use, and grammar books for foreign-language learners. Think what your requirements are and match them to the best book available.

Informal learning through discovery

The other way of learning takes longer but it can work well if you are surrounded by the language. In this approach you read and read as much as possible and you do as much listening as you can. Gradually the patterns of the new language become part of your thinking and your output in the same way as happened with your first language. You can test whether this is happening for you by referring to a grammar book and noticing how many of the 'rules' you are already applying, although you couldn't explain to anyone else why one way sounds right and the other sounds wrong.

If you are making the most of all the reading and listening resources available you are probably doing some informal learning without realising it. You can always supplement and speed up the process by adding some formal learning as well. Here's an example.

Let's say that you like the idea of discovering the patterns of the language, rather than looking up rules in the book all the time. In that case, while you are reading or listening to the new language try to focus on one particular aspect of the language, such as the way people link their ideas. This is likely to be different in speech and in writing. Photocopy a page, take some coloured felt-tip pens and use a separate colour for each device used for linking. Here are some to look out for:

> reference words (*this, that, which* . . .),
> content words and phrases (*although, provided that, since* . . .),
> repetition (the same word in the following sentences),
> synonyms (*the event, the happening* . . .).

Table 10.1 shows how you could organise your findings.

Here are some more ideas to go through with different aspects of grammar.

1. Clarify the problem you are having with a particular grammar point.
2. Ask someone else to explain the point.
3. Try explaining it to another student. Take turns at asking and explaining until the point becomes clear.
4. Look for further examples to verify or expand your 'rule'.
5. Distinguish between two similar grammar points ('It's not like . . .').
6. Try to work out a rule before looking it up.
7. Check your understanding from a reference book. Make connections between your understanding and the textbook explanation.
8. As well as looking for different sources, try reading the same sources over several times, preferably leaving time between them. Some aspects of language become clearer a second or third time.

Gradually in your notebook you will build up information about the connection between the form of the language and its use in many contexts: formal and informal situations, written and spoken language, narrative and dialogue, and so on. For example, students of English and

TABLE 10.1   HOW YOU CAN ORGANISE YOUR FINDINGS

Question	Ideas for finding answers
What are some differences between written and spoken language?	1. Collect a sample of one kind of language (a report, a narrative) from speech and from writing.
	2. Ask yourself questions: *What is similar about the two samples? What is different?*
	3. Start making notes in your own grammar notebook.
[Your question] [Your question]	

many European languages might notice that the passive voice is often used to describe a manufacturing process, while the past simple tense is common for biographies.

Reading and listening to explanations

Finding out grammatical patterns for yourself is just one way of learning the rules. One student writes as her main piece of advice for learning grammar, *'Listen in class.'* Ideally, your teacher will be helping to clarify for you the parts of the new grammar that give most trouble. Remember to ask questions. If you sit looking pleasantly receptive as teachers speak they may assume that all is well. Ask questions that identify your problem exactly. For example:

Is that the same as saying . . . ?
How do I know when to say . . . and when to say . . . ?
Could you explain again the bit about . . . ?

One student has some independent tactics for remembering grammar explanations, which involve making connections with what she has already experienced.

I try reading rules and memorising them, using my recollection of how I used to hear things spoken in Italy.

This led her to 'absorb' rules so that when it came to using the grammar she found it was a case of 'using my instinct sometimes as to what "fits" best in certain sentence constructions.'

Recording grammar patterns

The three most popular ways of recording grammar for later review seem to be: using coloured highlighters for grammar notes provided by the teacher or the textbook, abbreviating the notes, adding original examples, and finally, recording the grammar points graphically. You need to experiment with how to group the rules so you can find them later. One student recommended two notebooks, one with notes recorded in the order learned in class and a second for grouping together rules that belong together.

Graphics are a chance to use your originality. One student made up charts for verb endings in French. The example in Figure 10.1 shows how another one made a mindmap for a point in Spanish.

If you are like the student who can 'memorise photographically grammar tables and charts', you are one of the fortunate few who can recall and select bits of information at the right time. The person who was able to memorise also mentioned other stages such as 'writing and speaking sentences using a particular form/case/tense'.

Some students recommend making special notes on exceptions to the normal patterns. Others find that mnemonics help for irregular forms of verbs.

All grammar learning seems to be summed up as the search for patterns and the noting of exceptions. The search is easier in some languages and for some learners than others, as a student of French found.

> French grammar is quite systematic, so all I needed was the initial algorithm for conjugations and word syntax. Exceptions to rules were a matter of MEMORY and I have a good memory. Use of the language in all ways helped.

Describing grammar

One of the things you have to decide is how much it helps you to be able to use the language labels for describing grammar. Do you want to be

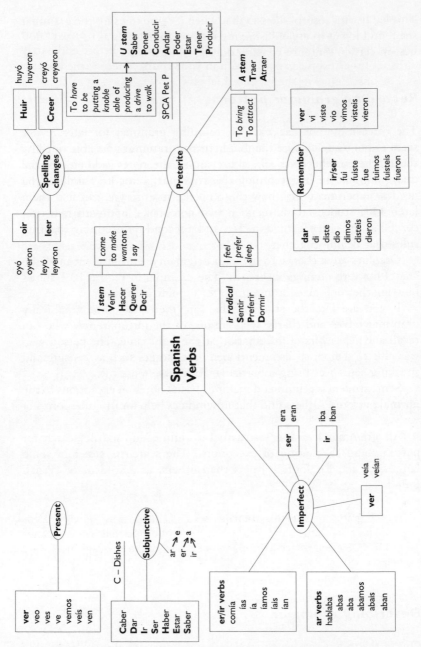

FIGURE 10.1 GRAMMAR MINDMAP FOR SPANISH VERBS

able to talk about the future perfect tense, active and passive verbs, the difference between adjectives and adverbs and so on? The answer will depend partly on the way you have learned languages before and partly on what other people expect of you in your course. Here is the case for and against knowing the technical labels.

For using grammatical labels

They are like the tools of the trade. Just as it helps to be able to call a spade a spade when you are asking someone to pass it to you, rather than calling it 'the metal thing for digging with a wooden handle at the top', so some people like to be able to describe language in quick, easily understood terms. A second reason has to do with using reference books. Most of these organise an index around labels and therefore you can find the entry faster. A third reason for some students is that the teachers are always using the grammatical labels and therefore it saves time in the long run to master them.

Against using grammatical labels

On the other hand, your interest may be entirely with using the language, including listening and reading other people's use of it, and the labels are unnecessary. You may have found a grammar book that doesn't use traditional labels and you may have a teacher who avoids them too.

To sum up the two points of view, if grammatical labels are going to be useful to you, learn them. If not, forget it. Whatever happens, a language student today is expected to be able to use the language. (For examples of grammar terms, see the end of Chapter 1.)

Questions about learning grammar

Should the learners' first language be used for language learning?

We have already seen that translation is used by some learners and their teachers as a means of thinking in detail about the new language. Another aspect of first-language use is as a language of explanation. For the beginning language learner their is no choice. If the teacher doesn't explain a grammar point in English then there can be no explanations and it must all be by discovery. Even in some more advanced classes the teacher will make explanation in the students' own language to save time and increase understanding. If some students believe that interrupting the flow of language spoils the learning process this will annoy them. On the other hand, if they believe that quick and comprehensible explanation of word meanings and tricky grammar points speeds things up then they will be pleased.

The same point applies to your choice of grammar reference book. For most languages there is a wide range available. Whether you choose one with explanations in English or in the target language will depend partly on your level and partly on the goals of your language learning. Reading explanations in the target language will be useful if you plan to do further language studies in a country where that language is spoken.

Should all my errors be corrected?

There is considerable debate amongst learners on the marking of assignments and on teachers' responses to students' class contributions. Some believe that having every error in speech corrected is important so that wrong forms will not become fossilised. Others are happy for the teacher to concentrate on a few errors of form only and to respond more to errors of fact. This second view is closer to the finding of current research in second-language learning.

10.2 PRACTISING GRAMMAR

We have already heard from students who meet with one another for language practice and from students who write out language on their own. All of them are finding opportunities to practise the form of the language. Some of the questions they ask about grammar practice are these:

Are grammar exercises a good idea?
How do I know if I'm making mistakes?
Is it important to have someone correct your writing?
Should I stick to the easy things I know how to say correctly?
Why do I keep making the same mistakes?

Let's consider some answers to these questions.

Grammar 'exercises'

The word 'exercise' suggests something mechanical, where the emphasis is on getting words in the right order, without thinking too much about meaning. That is not the kind of exercise that's useful to the intelligent language learner. Instead, think of practising new grammar patterns in a context where they make sense. In the words of a French student, 'Do lots of exercises after studying and understanding the concepts.'

At the beginner's level you could be writing short sentences about what you did last weekend. That way you are practising both the form and the vocabulary of the language. The paragraph you finish up with may be more boring than one you will write in a year or two but nobody needs to see it except yourself.

Of course, you could take this type of exercise a step further and write it in the form of a letter to another student, who will then write back some questions. The questions, too, are a type of exercise. They will be asking for information the questioner really wants to know but they will be based on a simple pattern. Here is an invented example in English.

At the weekend I phoned my friend.
He was at home.
I went to his house.
We took the bus to town.
We saw a movie.
Then we had coffee.

The questions could be just as simple:

Who is your friend?
Where does he live?
Which bus did you take?
What was the name of the movie?
Did you like it?
How much was the coffee?

This is not the stuff that novels are made of but at least it is communication at a level you can manage.

Another type of 'exercise' involves practising the patterns of a sentence, as in the example in Table 10.2, where a student sets up a pattern of the word order and then tries to write as many correct sentences as possible.

TABLE 10.2

Subject	Frequency	Verb	Direct Obsect	Place	Time
Doctors	rarely	visit	patients	in their homes	at night.
Children	often	ask for	ice-cream		at odd times.

The easiest sort of exercises are those provided by your textbook. Checking the answers as you go is important. You don't want to reach the end of one set and find that you've made the same mistake ten times. Many textbooks now provide answer guides at the end rather than in a separate teacher's book because people realise how important it is for students to be able to work through them at their own pace.

Getting and using feedback

Outside of class, the most natural way of finding out if you are making mistakes is from other people's responses. If the mistakes are too serious your listeners will be asking you all the time what you mean. If they are not so serious then people may be asking you whether you said such and such. That will tell you how close you are to speaking 'correctly'.

Of course, there are other times when it is important to have errors pointed out. Your class assignments are probably marked in this way, in which case you need to spend time going over them to take advantage of the individual feedback. In some classes the teacher gets better and better at grammar because she does all the corrections, but the students make slow progress if, when an assignment is returned, they quickly stuff it into their folders without looking.

You are the person who should be correcting your errors, even if the marker has signalled them. When you look at them, there are some steps to work through. One distinction that has been made about learners' language is this. You make mistakes about rules that you already know but you make errors about points you haven't learned yet. In other words, you can find your own mistakes, but not your errors. First, make sure you understand what you should have written or said, or your correction will simply be another stab at the right answer. Next, decide on the best way of practising the correct form. Would it help you to write out the sentence once more? Can you make up another, similar sentence? Then you could think of a way to test yourself in a few days' time to see whether you have remembered the right form. Anyone can get it right immediately after being told. The challenge is to remember it and apply it later.

Causes of mistakes or errors

If you are making mistakes, then you should congratulate yourself. The reason is that students who make plenty of mistakes are not letting themselves be held up in their communication by the fact that they are only at page 50 of the textbook. They just go ahead expressing their meaning in the best way they can. After all, if you don't learn how to complain until Chapter 20 of your course, does that mean you have to suffer everything that goes wrong until then? It may help you to identify the cause of some of the errors you are making. Table 10.3 gives some categories. You will need to think of examples from the language you are studying.

Teachers give different advice about how big a chunk of language students should memorise. There are some viewpoints in Table 10.4.

Techniques for practising grammar

Practise new structures
Make a conscious decision to write a paragraph using two or three new structures that you have learned recently. Use the textbook or grammar book as often as you need.

TABLE 10.3 CAUSES OF ERRORS

Cause of error	Example
1. This is a difficult point even for native speakers of the language.	
2. The difficulty is that in English these two points are not separated.	
3. The grammar point is very similar to a point in your own language but has a slightly different meaning or application.	

TABLE 10.4 ADVANTAGES AND DISADVANTAGES OF MEMORISING
LENGTHS OF LANGUAGE

Language chunk	Advantages	Disadvantages
Single words	Easily put on cards	No context
Phrases	Idiomatic speech Saves time	Don't know how common they are
Dialogues	Shows language in use	People you talk to don't stick to the words

Correct someone else's writing
All writers make use of proofreaders. You can carry out this role for a
fellow student, explaining to him or her exactly what is wrong. Explaining points to someone else improves your own understanding.

Analyse different types of language
Look at examples of the different types of writing you want to do: essay
writing, formal letters, e-mail correspondence. Start to notice the form
of the writing and think about what you could imitate.

Make comparisons with your language
Think consciously about differences between expressions in your own
language and in the one you are learning.

SUMMARY

To conclude this chapter, here is some advice.

1. Focus most of the time on the meaning of the language you are
   learning and only occasionally on the form.

2. Vary between looking at examples first and looking at rules first.

3. Think about whether the tactics you are using are helping you to
   understand the grammar, to record it, to practise it, to remember it
   or to use it in genuine communication.

4. Attend both to the patterns in sentences and to the patterns in longer chunks of language.

5. Look at examples from both written and spoken language.

6. Focus occasionally on difficult distinctions, e.g., 'When do I say . . . and when do I say . . . ?'

7. Use a variety of interesting ways of recording the new grammar for yourself.

11

READING FOR SEVERAL PURPOSES

> *Reading in a new language has two main purposes. Students read because they are interested in the content of the articles and books, and they read as a means of learning more language. Ideally, both these functions happen at the same time, as we see in this chapter.*

Right from the first day of your language learning you are likely to be doing some reading. Although some language-learning methods used to recommend not looking at the printed word until you had spent a long time listening and speaking, adult learners who have had a formal education find that having the printed word as a support helps their memory. This, by the way, does not apply to learners who have never learned to read and write a first language. They can learn plenty of language just by listening and remembering because they have highly developed skills for sounds rather than for print.

One factor that will influence what you want to get out of reading is the reason why you are studying the language (to read signs when you travel, to study science). You could be interested in any of these levels:

Basic literacy involving a new script.
Reading passages written for language learners.
Functional reading.
Reading for pleasure.
Reading for course requirements.
Reading literature written for native speakers of the language.

This chapter starts with some information about the process of reading in a new language. It then surveys the types of reading you could be doing and finally it gives examples of reading in action which you can practise.

11.1 THE PROCESS OF READING IN A NEW LANGUAGE

First- and second-language reading

First you need to be aware of the difference between learning to read and reading to learn. Assuming that you already read in your own language, and possibly others, you already know a great deal about the reading process which you won't have to re-learn. You know that the symbols convey meaning, you know they have to be read in a certain order on the page (although the direction could be different), and you know that there are certain patterns in written text which correspond to the sounds you hear when you listen, even if they don't correspond phonetically.

So what is new? If the language you are learning is more phonetically based than English (Italian, Spanish and Samoan, for example) then you are in for a pleasant surprise. What you see on the page and what you hear when people speak will correspond in a way that makes reading easier for beginners than it is in English. There are none of those tangles that the learner of English has to undo, such as the difference between *cough* and *rough*, *tough* and *trough*, not to mention *fort* and *fought*, or *taut* and *taught*. On the other hand, if you are learning a language like Chinese, where the symbols are not at all phonetically based, then one of the skills you used in learning to read English, sounding out words to see what made sense in the context, will not work. However, as we shall see, there is much more to reading than making sounds from symbols.

Another link with your first language is your attitude towards reading. If you have always enjoyed picking up a book or a magazine for pleasure or for information, then you will probably enjoy doing the same with your new language, once you have passed the initial stage. If books have been of less interest to you than other forms of entertainment then you will have to work more seriously at motivating yourself to read.

What makes reading difficult in a new language?

Learners report two main difficulties, which may be linked. There are too many unknown words and as a result reading is simply not a pleasure. For some students, even reading in their own language is a chore.

Lack of vocabulary

Having a wide vocabulary is essential to making sense of written language. Of course, this is a circular argument, because the more you read the more vocabulary you learn and the more words you know the more easily you can read. Don't make the mistake of reading with your dictionary beside you, looking up every single new or doubtful word. This is laborious and prevents you from practising the skill of prediction.

Sometimes in reading you find a word you know but the sense doesn't seem to fit in. This is not surprising because words have so many meanings and degrees of meaning. What is more, part of their meaning is shaped by the words around them. Keep looking at the surrounding words and asking yourself 'What sort of meaning would make sense here?'

Of course, at the early stages it is sometimes difficult to find material beyond the textbook written at a level you can read unassisted, although easy readers for adults are available in some languages. Here is what one student of French found:

> At first I was constantly searching the dictionary to make any sense of the written code, but eventually I got to the stage where I could read a sentence and basically understand it, so then I just started to read a lot, not worrying about certain words if I had grasped the basic meaning. Then the context dictated the meaning of these foreign words and my vocabulary grew.

His comments reinforce the point that knowing words helps your reading and reading helps the growth of your vocabulary. (See Chapter 7 for ideas about vocabulary learning.)

Lack of enjoyment

If you find reading tedious then of course you will do less of it. Here are some tips for making it more enjoyable.

1. Read at a manageable level. See if you can find graded readers prepared especially for language learners.

2. Choose reading that provides some support to meaning through glossaries or graphics. There are even a few bilingual books with English on one side and the new language on the other.

3. Turn reading into a group activity. Ask a couple of friends to join you. Each of you reads the same article or chapter and then you discuss the main ideas.

4. Read the kind of thing you enjoy reading in your own language, whether it is non-fiction (magazines, newspapers) or fiction (prose or verse), formal or personal writing. You might even find translations of comics. Tintin and Asterix books, for example, have been translated into many European languages.

Approaches to reading

The more that people study the reading process, the better they can pass on to language learners a range of advice to choose from. People have learned to read in all kinds of ways. Here is some information that could help you as you plan to be a better reader in the foreign language you are studying.

Work out the general meaning first

When people start to read in a new language they often feel they must take a detailed approach, focusing on every word, particularly those they don't know. They read as if they were using a microscope, looking carefully at each of the small pieces (the individual words), but not necessarily seeing the whole picture at first. This is called the 'bottom-up' approach. Other readers try to look first at the big picture (the 'top-down' approach), attending to individual bricks only as necessary, a process that involves some intelligent guesswork. Generally this second approach is recommended by successful learners.

When you go for the general meaning you have to do plenty of guessing. Guessing might remind you of random games where you have to think of a number and hope for the best. In reading, guessing is much more than that. It is predicting, which has a more logical sound to it.

You learn to predict meaning without having to think separately about each word. You then test and confirm your predictions by reading on and seeing if your guess makes sense. Here are comments from two students who were asked what techniques they used in order to read with understanding. Notice how they both move from general to specific meaning as they read.

> I skim through to get general meaning. I avoid lingering on single words I don't understand. Reading over things quickly and imagining (or speaking aloud) the sound helps to understand meaning especially for similarities in English words. [She studied Italian and Spanish.] I don't always concentrate on how it's spelt but how a word sounds, looking up difficult words in a dictionary.

> I had to learn to quickly read a whole text to get the sense of it, then read again more slowly working out the exact meaning and guessing what unfamiliar words might mean in the context.

One student, on the other hand, is not impressed by the advice to guess at meaning:

> I found when learning how to read Japanese that it was very important not to guess too much about unknown parts of the text. In fact, I would recommend to learners that they should aim to understand close to 100% of all texts that they study. The parts which are important (e.g. important expressions etc.) will stick because they tend to come up time and time again. If learners don't understand everything from class they should go to the library and look up dictionaries and grammar books etc. I think I was too dependent on the teacher in my first year or two learning Japanese at Uni and it didn't occur to me until my third year to go to the library and find useful books!

Reading is probably, as these students suggest, a combination of both processes. Ask yourself whether you need, at this moment, to spend more time on intelligent guessing or whether you are already doing plenty of that, and what you need is to allow yourself the occasional dive into a dictionary.

Interactive reading

Another way of thinking about reading is to describe it as an interactive process, where the text brings something to you and you bring something to the text. Readers bring together all their knowledge of the world with what they see on the page in front of them. That is why, when reading in our own language, we don't need to read every word. We add meaning which is not actually stated. Imagine that you read this sentence in the middle of a passage:

In he walked, wearing a hat.

One difference between you and the person sitting beside you is the sort of hat you picture. People put together their own knowledge of hats with the context they are reading about and come up with their own mental picture.

Then there are differences in people's reactions to the fact that the author has bothered to mention this detail. What does it add to the story? Either you will be surprised that the author even bothers to mention the hat ('What's so strange about that? Why didn't they mention all his other clothes too?'), or you will start assigning some meaning to the hat. Before you read on, try to think what reasons you might assume for the person to be wearing a hat:

He's going to a special ceremony.
He is being defiant of social conventions.
It's cold.
He forgot to take it off when he came in.
That's the custom where he lives.

The reason that comes to your mind before you find out the point the author wants to make, will depend on your knowledge of the world. That is one reason why it is easier (but more boring) just to read about familiar themes.

From supported reading to independent reading

Language learners start by needing considerable support as they read. Textbooks supply this support in the form of:

introductions that summarise the content,
glossaries,
pictures and diagrams,
explanations of new grammar points.

In your reading you need to move gradually from this support to reading more authentic texts.

11.2 TYPES OF READING

Let's look now at some of the types of reading you are likely to do in your language course.

Basic literacy

Reading and writing cannot be separated if you are learning a language with a new script. The process of reading will help to develop your writing skills and vice versa. You have to reach the point where you can do all the following:

1. Connect the sounds you hear with the symbols you see on the written page. Note that most terms in Chinese have two parts to the character: one for meaning and the other for sound.

2. Learn the special features that distinguish one character from another.

3. Read with understanding everything from basic functional signs such as the symbols for 'men' and 'women' in public places to more complex written messages such as personal letters.

4. Learn anything about the writing in the new language that has cultural significance.

5. Recognise differences between the written and spoken forms of the language.

6. In some languages, like Arabic, where the script goes from right to left, you also have to learn a different direction for eye and hand movement.

Reading aloud

In some language classes reading aloud is part of the lesson. Many students report that they read aloud to help them understand the text. It is easy to confuse the ability to pronounce words properly, with reading for meaning. Sometimes people can do one without the other. If the language is phonetic it is possible to put on quite a polished performance of reading aloud without having too much idea of what you are reading. While this may fool some people it shouldn't fool you.

There is not much point in reciting something you don't understand. As one student says,

> I read aloud over and over until I am reading and understanding at the same time. Not trying to translate the sentence into English.

Reading literature

The highest level of reading is probably reading literature as written for native speakers. In fact some people see being able to read literature as the main purpose of studying a language. The higher you go with your studies the more possible this is.

> In Stage 2 French I didn't do the literature papers and felt that put me at a disadvantage, so in Italian I did the literature papers.

The topic of reading literature is dealt with in the next chapter.

11.3 READING IN ACTION

Strategies for reading

Many strategies are the same in reading your own or another language, so that if you are doing plenty of reading already you will be doing these things.

1 Identify the type of writing

A good starting point is to think about the overall structure and purpose of what you are reading. You will know this partly from the title and partly from the place where you find the reading (a literature collection, a popular magazine).

2 Read many different types of material

Here are some examples of reading that eight successful language learners report reading. As you can see, there is a range in what particular students read, with some keeping to the textbook and others seeking out wider sources:

textbooks;
exercises, class work, magazines;

elementary material with a dictionary at hand;
books with translations on alternate pages;
magazines, song words;
novels, journals, newspapers, magazines, comics;
modern novels;
letters from penfriends, magazines, easy readers.

Although reading for meaning seems to make the most sense, students also reported just reading anything that would improve their language, including labels on food jars.

Here is one practical idea. Think of a theme that you want to find out about in depth. If it is also an assignment for your course then you will have even more impetus. Read about it from sources at different levels: summaries in weekly news magazines, longer editorials, books for children, technical books. Don't attempt to understand everything you read. You are aiming at getting both an overview and some details of the topic.

3 Work out your purpose for reading

Your purpose for reading will vary according to the type of reading and your course requirements. During a two-week period practise reading for different purposes: scanning for some information you want, skimming to get the gist of a passage, detailed reading for in-depth understanding. Some purposes and the strategies that are associated with

TABLE 11.1 PURPOSES AND STRATEGIES FOR READING

Purpose	Strategies
Read for overall meaning	Check title. Skim the text.
Read for details	Scan. Pose questions to yourself.
Read to find answers	Check topic sentences (often 1st).
Read to learn language	Look for learned language patterns. Look for new meanings. Note new vocabulary.

them are shown in Table 11.1. Details of skimming and scanning are given below.

The difference between skimming and scanning is this. When you skim read you are taking in big chunks of meaning at a time. The title has told you what to expect and the information you pick up as you look over the text should confirm the title. Scanning, on the other hand, involves looking for some particular items. It helps if you have some key words in mind while scanning, although, unlike electronic scanning of text on a computer, you can keep your eye open too for synonyms and paraphrases of those key words. When your purpose is to learn new language you may also need your reference books.

Choosing a dictionary

Your dictionary, like your grammar reference book, is one of the tools of your trade that will follow you through your language-learning career. Students refer to dictionaries in relation to their reading more than in any other aspect of their study:

> I read through the textbook and use a dictionary.

It is worth thinking about the type of dictionary you want, or perhaps types, as you work your way through the levels. Of course size comes into it. You may choose to have a pocket dictionary that follows you round through the day and a huge two-volumed one at home. If you opt for the latter, scan the second-hand bookshop for something reduced in price.

Medium is another consideration. As well as all the traditional print dictionaries, you can now choose from electronic versions. These range from the pocket types where you have just word-for-word translations to more sophisticated dictionaries on your computer. The price of the latter is often comparable with the printed versions and may offer greater flexibility such as being possible to upgrade at low cost to new editions when they are released, built-in search or thesaurus functions, or recorded pronunciation of words. In addition there are many on-line dictionaries on the Internet which you can use to translate words to and from a variety of languages.

Apart from the size and format, there is the question of level and language. Here are some types to choose from.

Bilingual dictionaries

Most learners want to start with a bilingual dictionary, in print or electronic form. These work fine for concrete items (car, tree, bicycle) and for easily translated concepts (son, anger, group) but after that they have their pitfalls. One student looked up just one meaning for fencing and couldn't make sense of something that turned out to be the sport, rather than the farm fencing. Many words have quite distinctive and different meanings. You will be able to think of examples from the language you are learning.

Check whether the dictionary includes a guide to pronunciation and whether you can understand that guide. For instance, are you familiar with the IPA (International Phonetic Alphabet), if those are the symbols the dictionary uses?

Monolingual dictionaries for language learners

Halfway between bilingual dictionaries and those written for native speakers of the language, there are dictionaries prepared for language learners. Ideally, these will include examples as well as definitions and explanations. Look for the features you want. Does the dictionary tell you which version of the language uses which word (e.g., European or South American Spanish)? Does it have pictures? Is the language of explanation at the right level for you?

Native speaker's dictionaries

If you are ready for one of these then you will have many advantages. You will be reading explanations and examples that take your language beyond simply telling you the meaning of a word. You may be finding out about the word's origins, about idiomatic uses. You would need to check, for some languages, whether the version you have takes account of regional differences in languages such as, for instance, the Spanish used in mainland Spain or in Latin America.

Summary of dictionary features

When you are choosing your dictionary, here, in brief are features to consider and questions to ask yourself.

1. Portability   Do you want to use the dictionary at home and
                     at school?
2. Pronunciation   How clear to you is the guide?
3. Examples   Are there plenty of actual examples with each
                     entry?

| 4. Level | Does the dictionary take you slightly ahead of your current level? |
| 5. Explanations | Are grammar, meaning and style all explained? |

Computer-assisted reading

We have already mentioned a number of uses for computer-based programmes in language learning. This resource is still under-used by many learners, simply because they don't know what is available. There is a gap between what is there and what students are aware of. Computers are being used at all stages of reading. For example, computers can:

1. Introduce symbols in scripts that are different from your own.
2. Provide practice in writing those scripts.
3. Offer a range of exercises, some mechanical and others with a focus on meaning.

Programs may already be installed on the computers at your school or university. If not, you could consider looking at catalogues to see what is available on CD-ROM.

Some people question whether computers can really help you to read, any better than picking up a book. There is some justification for this, but listen to the arguments from people who believe that computers have something to offer. The first argument relates to motivation. Anything that makes you spend more time reading will be helpful, so if you are someone who likes to turn on your computer as soon as you walk into your room, then you could find yourself motivated to spend more time on your foreign-language reading if it appears on your screen. There is more to computers than motivation, though. You need to make use of all the technical possibilities, because good programs allow things to happen which are not possible with a book.

This leads on to the idea of autonomy in language learning. We have already seen many times in this book that you, the language learner, will make a far bigger difference to your ultimate success than your teacher will. With a computer, *you* can decide how many repetitions to have and how to respond to the commands. In some programs you also shape the direction of the story you are reading by the selections you make. In other words, you don't have to move along at the pace of the rest of the class, which you may find too slow or too fast.

The flip-side of learner autonomy is learner misuse of programs. Some programs allow short-cuts which give you a sense of having finished, but without actually having done much learning. You need to be mature in your approach to the programs, remembering that, unlike a teacher, the computer doesn't care whether you finish the program in depth or superficially or not at all. At the end of a session using well-designed materials, you should have learned more than some new vocabulary and sentence patterns; you should also have learned more about the reading process – such as strategies of prediction, the use of context, and other skills which you can also transfer to your listening. As with all aspects of your language learning, you can finish your session with a critical eye to what you have learned from the program. This will include thinking about whether to repeat it or to move on to another level.

Here are some questions to ask about computer programs:

1. How many of the learning phases does this reading program support?

   Introducing new reading texts.
   Demonstrating strategies for reading.
   Checking understanding.

2. Is the program dependent on having a supervisor or is it simple to use? Is there a handbook accompanying it? What are the 'Help' and 'Clues' facilities? Are the 'What to do next' instructions displayed on the screen?

3. What forms of feedback are provided, beyond the messages 'Well done' and 'Sorry'?

4. What about the cultural content of the reading? Does the content deal just with superficial aspects such as clothes, names, homes and activities, or does it include the more subtle aspects of relationships and values?

5. What is the source of the texts? Are they authentic texts, modified versions of these, or have they been designed for language learners? Some modification has to happen to make the text comprehensible to students in their first year or two of study, but too much modifi-

cation results in artificial language. The more you can come to grips with authentic language the greater your sense of progress. Don't be put off by the difficulty. You can often use context as a clue to meaning.

6. How many different types of text are included – narrative, verse, non-fiction, or a combination of many types?

7. How does the program deal with language-learning aspects such as vocabulary development and new structures?

Measuring your reading progress

One way of finding out how well you are reading is by doing the traditional type of 'comprehension' exercise that appears in university examinations. There is a passage followed by questions, most of which can be asked directly from the text, with some requiring you to infer meaning that isn't actually spelled out. However, there are other ways of assessing your reading which you can do for yourself. Try some of these.

1 The enjoyment factor

It is important to ask yourself whether you are actually enjoying your reading because the more you enjoy it the more you will read. If you find yourself with an answer like 'I really hate the reading part of the course,' then it could be time to look at your motivation in general. (See Chapter 4 for suggestions.)

2 The understanding factor

Another aspect of your reading to check is how much you understand. Every now and then, follow up your reading of a chapter from a set text by trying to write a summary of the chapter. It doesn't matter whether you do this in a paragraph or a list or in note form. Next, check back to see if you have the main points. The big thing is to see whether you really are understanding what you read. Understanding involves putting the events into your own words rather than trying to memorise bits of language.

3   The range factor

One way of assessing your reading is to see the range you are doing. Try keeping a list of all your reading in the new language for one week. The amount is one thing, but the range reminds you of what kind of language you are being exposed to. For example:

> fiction/non-fiction,
> writing for language learners / writing for native speakers,
> prose/poetry,
> language for entertainment / functional language.

4   Keep a reading log

A reading log records all that you are currently reading about language, literature and the world.

5   Assess your prediction skills

A way to test whether you are reading individual words or chunks of meaning is to try finishing a sentence that continues over the page. Provided the subject matter is reasonably familiar, you should be able to do this fairly easily.

12

LITERATURE IN THE LANGUAGE COURSE

> *The study of literature is valuable for its own sake. In addition, when students are learning a foreign language it serves multiple purposes. It introduces them to new ways of thinking and viewing the world as well as providing them with extensive passages of language in a range of contexts. This chapter explores the purposes for studying literature in the language class and suggests some ways that students can use literature to improve their general language development.*

12.1 WHY STUDY LITERATURE?

Literature is defined here as works written for native speakers of the language. In most language courses this means reading them in the original version, although publishers sometimes produce simplified versions to introduce language students to works of literature. We'll look now at three reasons why literature is worthwhile. If you are fortunate you will feel that all three apply to you.

Literature improves learners' language

If you are being introduced to literature in your language class then one purpose is to improve your own command of the foreign language. This works particularly well if the passages you are being asked to read are slightly beyond your own current reading level. If they are too easy they do nothing to build up your language, although they may serve the

197

other two purposes. If they are too difficult it becomes like a mathematical exercise of decoding symbols.

As with reading in general, you can take two approaches to your reading of literature. You can go for the broad picture first and then come back to concentrate on the details or you can start from the details. When you come to analyse the language, your tactics will depend on your level. For the beginner level, most of the advice in the last chapter will apply, but for more advanced students, what sort of language could you be learning?

You could analyse the style of the passages, asking the same sort of questions as you do when studying your own language:

How does the writer create an effect through language?
What are the overall patterns that differ from patterns in, say, short stories in your own language?
How does the writer move from one section to another?

Analysing the style will involve looking at the effect the writer was trying to create. What happens to build up tension, to sustain interest, to bring surprises? How does the language change according to who is speaking to whom? If your literature classes include talking about the literature you will need the language for doing this. In some literature classes this happens in the students' first language; if not, you will be introduced to the technical language needed to talk about metaphors, imagery and so on.

At a higher level still, you may be able to make comparisons between the language of one piece of writing and other literature you have studied. Comparative literature studies are now part of many university courses for students who read in two or more languages.

Literature is a source of information

A second reason for reading literature is for the messages it has for readers. If this is an important reason for you, then before you start reading a passage make a note of some questions you want the story or chapter to answer for you. The title should be your starting point for questions but sometimes you also have to read the first paragraph before you can think what it is you'd like to find out.

After you have read the passage once or more you will be able to exchange more information in class. What does the passage add to your understanding of literary tradition in this period and time? At a more personal level, how do the experiences of the characters here compare with your experience of life and the experiences of people you know? Have you learned something that will help you in your communication with native speakers? This could include language and topics for conversation.

Literature is entertainment

The third reason for reading literature is the usual reason why you go and get reading material in your own language from the library. It is a form of entertainment, parallel with watching a play, ballet or movie or listening to a music concert. If this is an important reason for you, don't be restricted by the books on your list. Overcome the enemy, time, by taking out bundles of reading for the holidays. Separate it from your work. Go and lie in a field or by the sea to read. Take no notes and don't ask yourself whether the book will be in a test when you get back. You are taking a step towards using literature for the purpose it was intended.

Build up your personal library with titles that will stand the test of time. Ask for books from your relatives for Christmas and birthdays, especially if you know people who are travelling and can find you unusual titles from other countries.

Then, instead of having just loosely structured conversation groups with your friends, organise into occasions for exchanges about what you have been reading. Talk about your responses to the literature as much as what it actually says.

12.2 MAKING THE MOST OF YOUR LITERATURE STUDY

Barriers to enjoying literature

Although it might sound negative to include a litany of problems in a section on enjoying literature, acknowledging problems is the first step to overcoming them. Here are aspects that students say are difficult about foreign-language literature.

1   The background references are unfamiliar

This is, of course, a common situation. If you are reading a short story about life in a Chinese village or a novel set in nineteenth-century Russia, then naturally there will be many unfamiliar references. One piece of advice is not to try and understand everything immediately. Let the world you are reading about build up gradually as the author paints a picture for you of another time and place. If you have ever read stories to young children you will know that they can get enjoyment out of a story even when they don't understand all the references.

2   Having to answer an exam question on it destroys the pleasure

People don't say that about going for their driving licence. The test is just a hurdle along the way to all the pleasure the car is going to be to you later. Perhaps at this moment the examination seems like more of a struggle than a way of enjoying literature, but long-term there is another world opening up to you.

3   It's not the language of real life

It's true that the way people speak in some kinds of fiction and poetry are not the ways you would need to speak on your first day in a country. On the other hand, when you come to communicate with people in those countries, you will be surprised at the overlap between literary and conversational language.

Reading poetry

If you enjoy reading poetry in your own language, you are part way to enjoying it in another. If you don't, then here's your chance to try again, because poems are usually short, quite concise pieces of writing which reveal more and more of their meaning as you re-read them. There is no 'right' way to read a poem but here are some suggestions.

1. Get a feeling for the poem by making sure you understand the title (at least its literal meaning), by checking the name and dates of the poem and by reading any introduction provided in the book.

2. A different approach is to ignore the title (which may be quite obscure anyway) and simply read the poem through, putting your own general meaning to it first.

3. Read the poem aloud to get the benefit of whatever sound effects the poet intended.

4. Ask a native speaker to read the poem to you with feeling. Check whether recordings of the poem are already available in your audio-visual library.

5. After the first reading, start to think about possible messages the poem has for readers. Consider whether the message could be different according to the reader's circumstances.

6. Ask yourself what language devices the poet has used to create particular effects. Look for examples where a number of meanings are possible because of the way the words have been put together.

7. Underline the words you *do* know first. What overall impression do they create? Then use your dictionary to probe the meanings of the other words. You will need more than a small pocket dictionary for most poetry.

8. Include the discussion of a poem in your reading with other students for informal language practice. Although discussing abstract ideas in the new language is not easy, it works if everyone is patient as they wait for the speakers to get their ideas out.

Reading a novel or short story

Let's imagine that you are reading a short story or you have been assigned one chapter from a novel to read for next week's tutorial. Whichever is your main reason for reading it, meaning is going to be vital.

1   Look at the title

What clues are there here? If the answer is 'None at all,' then perhaps there is a key word in the title that you need to look up first. Beware of imagery though. If you are using a small dictionary it may give you a literal meaning that doesn't allow for any plays on words that the writer may have intended.

2   Check the background

When and where is the author writing? What do you know about that time and place? What else have you read about the same period that could help fill in the picture for you?

3   Start reading

Try not to stop every time you meet a new word. Keep picturing the scene you set up for yourself from your answers to the questions in 1 and 2. Adjust the picture as more details come to hand, but don't expect to understand everything. Remember that even when you are reading fiction in your own language you expect the writer to play some unexpected tricks.

4   Concentrate on meaning

As you are reading, do some sketching that helps you keep the factual details in mind. The sketching could be a 'map' of the relationships between the characters, or a geographic map of the area. Note key names and dates so that these details don't confuse you.

5   Record your learning

Write down one thing you have learned from your reading. It could be something factual, or something to do with the language, or something more personal. Like your notes on the relationships and your map of the place, these could be useful later for your examination revision.

Conclusion

In a word, literature can be both the most rewarding and the most frustrating aspect of your study. We have already mentioned bilingual books as one form of support for beginners. Much as they are frowned on in some circles, many learners also report that simple versions of the classics, either in the language itself or translated into English, are invaluable. Lecturers are usually more enthusiastic about movie versions of literature. They have the advantage of making the writing more comprehensible, and if well done they also build up an image of the context. The various embassies in your country could be a source for these movies and your university video library probably has a collection too.

13

WRITING IN A NEW LANGUAGE

> *Because writing is the aspect of language use most frequently measured in examinations it is worth working at your written expression, even if you intend to do much more speaking than writing later. Whether you are learning a new language script or using the familiar Roman alphabet to express your ideas in another language, learning to write is far more than translating ideas from one language to another.*

Starting with functional literacy, and moving up through writing as a form of language practice to writing for a variety of purposes and in a variety of styles, this chapter combines information about how people learn to write with practical advice for language learners.

13.1 LEVELS OF WRITING

Functional literacy

In the last chapter we talked about the connection between reading and writing in basic literacy. If you are planning to travel during your university holidays to a country where the language is spoken, you will have a chance to practise your literacy at the most basic and functional level. You may have to

write notes to hotel personnel,
fill in forms (government departments, hospitals, etc.),
write down personal information.

So much for the real use of language. Let's consider now the steps by
which you will get there.

If you are learning to use a new script you will start by becoming
familiar with the unusual symbols. For some students this is half the fun.
They enjoy the appearance of the symbols even before they can associate
them with meaning. When it comes to producing the symbols there is
no substitute for practice, either on paper, or using one of those computer programs that take you through the direction of the handwriting.
You then trace the symbol via the cursor along with a moving image. As
you write you could follow the pattern of

look–say–write

so that sound and sight come together. Many successful students mention the time it took to master a new set of characters and the need for
repetition. This is how two students say they managed:

> Repetitive writing for Chinese characters.

> No technique really, just did a lot of it (writing).

One very successful student of Japanese pointed out that although
he put in time to practise the Japanese characters after he had
learned them he didn't need to continue this type of repetitive practice.
Another speaks of the time it took to learn to write in each type of
script.

> Lots of practice in the beginning, especially in Japanese.

> Mass repetition of characters.

> Looking the word up in my character book to identify how it is made up or
> looking it up in the dictionary.

Repetition was only part of the story though. Students emphasise the
importance of meaning. Making sentences is one of the preferred ways
of practising writing. Even before the sentence stage, though, there is
plenty of meaningful writing you can do to practise the basic script.
Here are some ideas.

1. Labelling maps makes you familiar with places that you will be reading about later.

2. Write out lists of items, such as shopping lists or reminders of simple tasks to be done through the day. This is also a way of practising simple vocabulary items without having to fit them into a structure.

3. This could lead to a simple diary of events through the week.

4. Why not write notes to other students? These could be invitations, comments or questions.

5. Some poems can be written with quite basic vocabulary and structures.

Finally, you could try to give one another short dictations, taking turns to choose sentences from the textbook or even to make some up for yourself.

Intermediate level writing

After a year or so, you are able to write with meaning. Whether the writing is assigned by the teacher or whether you develop some writing tasks for yourself, which many successful students do, your focus is no longer on getting the shapes of the letters right. Often the context for the meaning is work set as part of the course, as in one Italian course.

> I did the set essay each week, using a dictionary to check vocab., and trying out new verb forms.

Notice how this student sees the weekly essay as a chance to try out new language rather than to stick with the patterns she is sure she knows. Another mentions going beyond what you can do perfectly:

> Apply the rules as much as possible but in the end write the way you feel something would be written and get it corrected. Learn from your mistakes.

'Re-use structures seen in class' was common advice amongst the students. You can also include the structure in your regular writing.

> Try to incorporate the styles and techniques being learnt in class into my writing, i.e., if I saw a structure in an article I read I tried to use it in my own work. This greatly improved my style.

One way of doing this, which is slightly artificial as far as meaning goes but does give you practice in something difficult, is to see how many *true* sentences you can write using the same structure. For example:

> If only . . . then . . .
>   If only we had a ladder, then we could climb in the window.
>   If only nations could communicate then we wouldn't have so
>   many wars.
> People used to . . . but now they . . .
> People used to write letters but now they use the phone more.
> People used to think computers were for adults but now they buy
>   them for children.

Another student recommends:

> Learning set phrases and grammar structures.

Advanced writing

When you reach an advanced level you face the same processes as you do in your first language. This means that people who are already good writers in their own language tend to be good writers in the new language once they have the language to do it with. There are differences though.

Learning to write for a particular audience, say an academic audience, involves taking on the cultural traditions of that discipline. One example that changes from one language group to another is the place of the individual voice. For instance, if you are learning an Asian language at an advanced level the emphasis may be on acknowledging what scholars have said on a subject rather than on what you think. Individualism is viewed differently in different traditions.

Contrastive rhetoric is the study of differences in the rhetoric of writing in different languages. If you advance your language studies, that is one area to study, particularly if you are also studying translation. In some languages an essay (or a business letter) follows a direct path from introducing a topic to summing it up at the end, whereas in other traditions you might move around the topic for some time before actually announcing it. An argumentative essay is a good example. If you are presenting two viewpoints and then coming to some conclusion, you need to know whether the language you are using normally presents all the ideas on one side first and then all the others, or whether the tradition is to move between the two sides for each of several points.

All of this means that you cannot simply think of your ideas in one language and transfer them to another. However, when it comes to writing about complex ideas, there is some evidence that discussing ideas first in your own language is a good preparation for writing. If you are writing an advanced essay in, say, French, it could help you to talk about the ideas first in English, which is certainly not to say that you should write it out in English and translate it. What you are doing is sorting out your ideas, so that a lack of vocabulary in French doesn't hold the ideas back. The discussion clarifies the ideas first, separating the tasks of coming to grips with the ideas on the one hand, and expressing them in the new language on the other.

13.2 GENERAL ADVICE

People have different ideas about how to improve writing in a foreign language. Some say the big thing is just to start writing, and the more you write the more fluent and error-free you will become, particularly if your lecturer gives you helpful feedback on your assignments. This approach is called 'process writing'. Others say it is really important to study the style of the writing you want to imitate. This approach is called 'genre writing'.

Learn to write by writing

The process approach is based on the assumption that it is through attention to meaning, and not just form, that language – and writing – improve. If your lecturers/teachers are keen on this approach they may recommend diary writing, which they collect and respond to. They will probably pay more attention to your ideas than to your language, ignoring any 'mistakes' in grammar or usage. Journals which, as we have seen, you keep for yourself with nobody else seeing them are another way of improving the actual process of writing.

One advantage of diary or journal writing is that, unlike essay writing, you are not limited to one format or one topic. There is no introduction or conclusion to think about. You can write your thoughts in the form of statements or questions. You can describe something you have just heard and then switch immediately to saying you feel hungry. The choice of topic is yours.

Furthermore, there is no such thing as a plan, followed by a rough draft, a revised edition and then the final copy. The essence of journals and diaries is that they are spontaneous. If you feel like looking up a word you can, but otherwise you can adapt the language you do have to fill the gap. This freedom helps students who find that their biggest problem in writing in a new language is getting started. 'Writer's block' means that some are held up by lack of ideas, others by the need to think of a good opening sentence when they are writing in a more formal way.

In free writing your starting point can be anything. For example:

1. Stare at a postcard and write about it. A more sophisticated approach would be to start reflecting about the life of the painter or the events shown in the postcard.

2. Use your most recent vocabulary list as the basis for writing a paragraph that includes as many new words as possible.

3. Play music as background inspiration.

Study good writing

A different approach to writing is based on the belief that conscious attention to the form of the language leads to an understanding of and then fluency in a particular genre. This approach favours plenty of 'marking' by the teacher and plenty of access to good language models. You may have to seek these out from senior students, because many university departments do not like giving out samples of other students' work.

Learn from the lecturer's feedback

Whichever way you approach your essay writing, let's assume that it comes back marked. What do you do with your marked assignments? The way the marking is done may be out of your hands, but if your teacher does return your work with detailed comments and corrections, then you still have to decide whether to take any notice of them. It is easy to have as your main concern the grade you have been given, ignoring the remarks the teacher wrote or said.

Here are some uses you can make of feedback.

1. Make a mental note to follow the bits of advice next time.
2. Make an actual note of the advice under headings that will be useful next time.
3. Identify unclear comments and ask the teacher for an explanation.
4. Rewrite the essay using the feedback as a guide.

For example, Figure 13.1 shows a version of one lecturer's comments to advanced language students who had just written an essay that involved putting together information from many sources.

If you have helpful feedback then you can act on it, but many students, when they receive a poor mark for an assignment, have difficulty in identifying what the problem is. Is it their ideas, their vocabulary, or their writing skills that have let them down? You may need to ask the teacher which is holding up your writing.

CLASS FEEDBACK ON YOUR ASSIGNMENTS

Here are some of the features I noticed in each category of mark.

A-grade assignments
These went beyond mere description of the topic. The writers were able to read and synthesise information from many sources and then offer some critique with reference to the theory. They wrote so that it was easy to read without constantly turning pages back and forth to grasp the point. Also, the style was at a language level appropriate for this course, with quotations integrated into the text. These people used the conventions of referencing.

B-grade assignments
The B essays did a good job of bringing together theory and examples. The writers had done adequate but not extensive reading and for the most part made clear connections between the theoretical points and the classroom examples. Their style was generally easy to follow.

C-grade assignments
These essays had some or all of the following features, which can easily be attended to:

● Too few references, including no reference to one of the books on the topic.
● References listed at the end but not mentioned internally.
● Style that made reading difficult.
● Overall organisation unclear.
● No proofreading and/or editing.
● Disproportionate amounts of anecdotal material.

FIGURE 13.1

13.3   PRACTICAL IDEAS

Let's consider now the writing study you can organise for yourself without any suggestions from your lecturer.

Ask other people for feedback

One successful student of Indonesian and Japanese did not wait for her work to be marked by the teacher:

> I have some native speaker to mark my writing.

Another roped in a fellow student.

> A friend of mine who was also studying French would swap her writing assignments with me. We would read each other's and discuss them.

Make up writing tasks

Students worked out ways of multiplying the amount of writing they do.

> I kept my personal diary in French.

A student of Chinese and Japanese suggests:

> First, write a whole passage before lecture.
>
> Second, after lecture write down again the whole passage.

Others have these ideas:

> I write small memos (e.g., schedule for tomorrow).
>
> I religiously copied and examined the dictées we were given in class. This really helped my written grammar as well as my perception of sounds.
>
> I try to retell an incident.

Work cooperatively, via the computer

Having two or three students around the same word processor making suggestions for improving the text can work well. Someone can always come up with another idea or some more details on the last idea.

Real practice via e-mail, the Internet and penfriends

E-mail is halfway between writing and talking. Make use of e-mail. It is like speaking in its informality and need for quick response but like writing in that one could do it without any attention to intonation, or accent.

Another way you can use the Internet is to find penpals. There are many sites which list people all around the world who want to communicate with people in other countries. Most of these sites tell you which country the other person is in, what their interests are, and who they would like to communicate with. By using these sites you can contact people from the country whose language you are learning and practice the language with them.

Rewrite passage in a different style

After reading a passage written in one style, say journalese, rewrite it in another style as if you were writing a letter. This gives you a chance to see whether you really have understood the passage rather than just being able to do a summary using the original language.

Generate ideas for your assignments

When you have an assignment to do, spend some time with other students talking about the topic. This will ensure that you are on the point and have thought of as many angles as possible.

Write from topic sentences

This is an expansion of the last idea. You each write a series of topic sentences with plenty of space after them. Then pass the paper to someone else and ask them to write the next sentence. Using a prompt-list is helpful if you are really stuck, e.g. 'Add an example', 'think of an exception'. Try expanding this into a series of topic sentences:

Long, long ago this area was covered in forest.

Conclusion

Some of the ideas here may not have appealed to you. Strategies are very individual. If you have thought up a good idea and it has worked for you once, then it's worth passing on. This chapter ends with a list of strategies for better writing, from one student:

Writing using simple language, keeping a daily diary in Italian, getting someone to check what I wrote, thinking in Italian when writing and not translating literally from English, saying things over in my head to make sure they sound right, checking spelling using a dictionary.

14

CULTURE AND LANGUAGE LEARNING

What exactly do people mean when they talk about the culture of a particular language group? How much of the target culture do students of a language need to know to make progress? Can language students learn about culture without actually visiting the country? Should they try to learn about culture directly or pick it up through the rest of their language studies? This chapter suggests answers to these questions.

14.1 WHAT IS INVOLVED IN STUDYING CULTURE?

Definitions of culture

First, what is meant by culture? The *Collins English Dictionary* has a long list of definitions. Here are two of them:

the total of the inherited ideas, beliefs, values, and knowledge, which constitute the shared bases of social action

the total range of activities and ideas of a group of people with shared traditions . . .

If we translate those items into aspects of culture that a language learner needs to come to terms with we could include some of these things:

customs that go back centuries,
literature written over many centuries,
architecture and the influences on it,

213

traditional ceremonies,
movies, music and art from yesterday or today,
the way people relate to one another in families,
the values that are important to a society,
the sense of humour that people share.

You could make a much longer list just by thinking of all the things that
are important to the culture you were born into.

Why learn culture?

As a language student there are several reasons why learning about
cultural aspects is important and fun. One is interest. Knowing about
the way people behave makes your reading more interesting. Another
reason is usefulness. It's no good knowing the language if you don't
know how to behave when you talk. The fascinating thing about culture
is that there is always something new to learn. The people who speak
one language do not all think and act the same.

If you are going to have conversations with native speakers of a
language you need to know the sort of topics that interest them once
you get past 'Hello'. You need to know something about their favourite
sports, the current government of countries where the language is
spoken, writers, and outstanding national events in recent times, to
mention a few.

The way people think is closely bound with language. This is not the
place to give a long account of the relationship between thought, culture
and language but here are a couple of points. Languages are one channel
through which different cultures present their ideas both within their
own groups and in contact with others. The fact that a language does not
have the same range of words for particular distinctions as another
language does not mean that they do not value those things as much.

Whether or not your main intention in signing on for a language
course is to learn about people's cultural background, you will be learning
about it indirectly from some of the sources listed later in this chapter.

Pitfalls in understanding other cultures

When you are reading your textbook and looking at the illustrations, or
when you are watching movies, it is very easy to fall into traps. Here are
some to look out for:

Generalising from examples in textbooks and films

It is easy to think that everyone speaks, acts and dresses like the characters in textbooks. Just as films made in and about your country don't summarise your whole nation or even reflect the parts of it that you know well, so you can't expect the same from your textbook. Nowadays most people would realise that the huge differences within each society make it difficult for textbook writers to summarise one group of people. We have come a long way since the writers of a book written for learners of English who were going by ship to Australia in the 1950s tried to prepare the immigrants for what they would see. During the five-week sea voyage from Europe, they were told the following about the clothing of Australian men.:

> Men often wear grey, brown or navy blue suits; blue, grey or white shirts; black or brown shoes, and grey or brown hats. These colours are not bright. Men wear shirts and shorts or bright colours only at the beach.[1]

Apart from giving us an interesting glimpse of the streets of Sydney half a century ago, this short passage is a good reminder of how difficult it is to sum up even a description of typical clothing in a couple of sentences.

Limiting culture to one country

Another pitfall is to forget how many different groups of people might speak the language you are learning. Many of the foreign languages taught in English-speaking countries are spoken by groups of people who vary from one another just as dramatically as people who speak different languages. One of these differences is geographic. If you are learning Spanish you may be exposed more to the culture of mainland Spain than to South American cultures, or vice versa. For Chinese you are probably (but not necessarily) learning Mandarin, but if you plan to travel beyond the People's Republic of China then you want to know about the cultures of Taiwan, Hong Kong and Singapore. If you are learning Hindi are you planning to use it in India, or Malaysia or Fiji? In the more than 100 years since their ancestors moved to these countries, the Hindi language has undergone all the changes that happen to languages everywhere.

Remembering ethnic minorities

Another difference is between citizens of the same country. In many countries with a history of colonisation, the most popular language for foreigners to learn is the one spoken by the majority of the population, or in some cases not the actual majority but the group whose language is used for education and government. If you plan to visit these countries you will want to find out something about the lives of the indigenous people as part of your study. What is their status? What is their first or second language?

Gaining a superficial view of the new culture

Particularly in the early stages of language learning, when you can't enjoy the literature in its original form, it is easy to fall into the trap of seeing only the superficial aspects such as people's physical appearances, the clothes they wear and the average size of the family. The more you are able to understand the language, the further you can delve into more subtle aspects of the culture.

Noticing aspects of the culture that are different from your own is a natural starting point. We all view the world through our own 'spectacles'. On the other hand, the more you read and see the more you become aware too of universal threads in culture, including, for example, the fact that emotions are universal but that the way they are expressed varies around the world.

Glorifying the new culture

It is easy to go through a phase where you think of the new culture as having everything that is good or missing from your own culture. That doesn't matter if it acts as a motivation to keep learning but it can lead to disappointment when you actually visit the country.

Seeing a culture as static

Cultures change with the generations. The only aspects that are fixed for ever are the displays put on for tourists, who pay to see something different and traditional. Sometimes a language teacher has left his or her country years ago and may generalise on the basis of how things were then. One way to take change into account is to notice, through reading, through watching movies and through first-hand contact, how different generations act.

Blaming misunderstandings on cultural differences

Don't assume, once you start to communicate with people, that all the miscommunication that arises is due to cultural differences. If that was true you would never argue with (or fail to understand) people from your own culture. When two people talk, there are many reasons why there can be communication problems.

14.2 SOURCES OF INFORMATION ABOUT CULTURE

Your sources of information about culture are likely to be the same as you are using for the rest of your course, including:

> your course book,
> films,
> the news on TV or radio,
> literature,
> tourist brochures and posters.

Many other sources, such as magazines in your Departmental library, the Internet, international visitors, and newspapers (particularly letters to the editor and cartoons), are mentioned throughout this book. Let's see what these different sources offer.

The course book

Your language course book should be an important source of information about the life of people who speak the language you are learning. Textbooks take one of three approaches.

They may have explicit information about events and people. This option is the one taken by the 1950s textbook quoted earlier. It is also used in courses that target particular groups of people, such as business people, who are learning the language with a specific goal in mind. Explicit cultural information can be helpful for things like population size and the names of leaders, but less reliable if it tries to summarise what people believe and think. For example, if you are learning a new script, some of the factual explanations about the history of that script will be interesting as part of the language's cultural background. On the other hand it can lead to over-simplification when writers try to sum up, for example, what seems humorous in one country or how different family members relate to one another.

Another, more subtle approach is that the information is there but you have to read between the lines to see it. This option works well for students who have some idea of cultures beyond their own and who are good at drawing inferences.

Thirdly, the target culture may be ignored altogether in a textbook or course. This last option is unlikely in a serious language programme. It is not useful to be able to say the words of a language if you don't know anything about the contexts where they will be used.

Films

Few of us would want our lives to be judged entirely by the way people from our countries are portrayed in movies and yet students report spending quite a bit of time watching foreign-language movies as a means of language learning. At the same time as watching they must also be picking up messages about culture. For one thing, they find out the sort of subjects people think are worth making movies about. Try and discover whether a film was produced inside or outside the country. In some cases, the fact the movie has not been passed by the censors in the country where the language is spoken may mean the movie tells us something about standards and values which are not part of the official government line.

The news

One of the values of listening to and watching the news in a foreign language is that you start to be aware of wider viewpoints. This is particularly true of the big international debates. What slant do various nations put on the current debates about ecology, trade agreements, territorial disputes? The viewpoints expressed have developed from centuries of the other country's history, so the more you read of their history the better you understand their current viewpoint, and vice versa.

Literature

In some courses, language and literature are taught concurrently, in which case your teachers will be making connections for you between literature and culture. If you have the choice of whether or not to study the literature, then think of the advantages for your culture learning as well as for your language learning. You may even be reading the work of writers whose work has been banned in their own country, in which case the insights you have into particular topics may be greater than those of the citizens of that country.

Poetry, which some say is the most difficult area of literature to appreciate in a foreign language, is very dependent on culture to be understood. As you start reading poetry you will find answers to questions about both language and people.

What are the sources of the metaphors in the poem?
What sort of people in society are being written about?
Are the themes universal or country-specific?

See Chapter 12 for more on the subject of literature.

Travel brochures

Travel brochures are a good source of information about a country if you are about to be plunged into a holiday visit, or if you are going to interpret for people doing business there. They may give you some advice, such as guidelines for dressing on temple visits and information about times when you can and cannot expect to find the shops open.

14.3 CULTURAL KNOWLEDGE FOR PARTICULAR CONTEXTS

The use you plan to make of the new language will determine which particular aspects of culture interest you most. Here are examples of how culture affects five particular aspects of life: studying at an overseas university, home stays, writing business letters, having a job interview, and the workplace in general.

University study in different countries

If you are fortunate enough (or if you are working day and night to earn the money), you may include some 'study abroad' as part of your language-learning experience. This section is written for you. As well as all the general aspects of the culture that you have learned, you need to know about cultural aspects of university study in the country of your choice, and in particular how their practices differ from your own. It is easy to find out the broad facts such as the length of the course and the timetable but your concerns have to go further. Here are some questions you could ask.

1. How do staff and students relate to each other?
    Do students use lecturers' first names?
    Do they give gifts to lecturers?

2. What are the traditions for writing essays?
    What are the main sources for essays: class notes, readings, library resources?
    What are the differences in essay styles between your language and this one?

3. What are the traditional learning styles?
    How important is listening?
    Do students learn cooperatively or competitively?

4. Tutorials
    How do students get turns in tutorials?
    Is it polite to interrupt if you have something to say?

It is difficult to talk and act in ways that go against your preferred means of communication in a tutorial. A university student says,

> I don't join in discussions during tutorials because I'm not sure how to get a turn. The other students probably imagine I don't know anything about the subject. When I asked the tutor what the rules of conversation were in tutorials he said, 'Just interrupt. We do it all the time.' They may do it but I don't want to sound rude.

Home stays

Linked with studying in another country is the question of where you will live. Staying in a home gives you close contact with people's everyday lives and can be a great experience for learning in the most direct way possible. It can also lead to misunderstandings when the hosts are living by one set of rules and the international student by another.

Here is one example of not knowing what to do. A student tells her home-stay hostess that she didn't know how to turn away a salesman who had knocked on the door. The hostess's answer is simple, 'Next time just say "no thank you" and shut the door in his face.' The student feels this is extremely rude. She wants to be able to practise her own codes of politeness and yet achieve her aim of getting rid of the visitor.

Of course this is not the place to describe in detail what to expect in each country, but based on the experience of many people in many countries, here are some situations where there are likely to be differences in home living.

Arrangements for personal laundry.
Bathtimes, bedtimes, times for rising.
Use of power for various purposes (music, hairdriers etc.).
Telephone calls inward and outward.
Forms of address between different generations.
Gift giving.
Table 'manners'.
Visiting the homes of the host family's friends.

If you have been living in a hostel with all sorts of people from all kinds of backgrounds you may think this has been a good preparation for staying with a family whose life is very different from yours, but there is plenty more to learn. See if your school or university has booklets with information about the host country you are going to. If not, try the embassy or consulate in your own country before leaving. In particular be aware of differences that could arise if you are going from a relatively wealthy economy to one where families do not have goods that you have taken for granted. Vice versa is usually not such a problem. Most students find they can settle into a wealthier lifestyle without too much trauma.

The business letter

There are many special uses of language which you will learn if you advance with your studies. For the moment, let's look at one area (business language) and one particular task (writing a business letter). Even if you don't need to write a business letter yourself, as a language student you may be asked occasionally to help someone else write one. Remember that you can't simply translate from one language to another. Here are examples of different conventions.

1. Cultures differ in the topics that are and are not appropriate in a business letter. For example, should you mention anything personal?
2. There are differences too in how spontaneous or fixed the language is.
3. What sounds like taking a pleasant personal interest in the client in one culture may sound insincere or inquisitive in another.
4. Sometimes the language of the business letter is close to everyday speech; elsewhere it is much more formal.

Start collecting examples which you can use as a model, or get hold of a book on the topic.

The job interview

Job interviews are another minefield. Many students travel to another country in their holidays and, provided they have the right passports or visas, they are able to take short-term jobs. These are a way to practise your language skills on the spot, not to mention earning money to pay for the rest of your studies. Some of the preferred jobs are in the tourist industry, such as waiters and waitresses, tour guides and ski-resort workers.

The first step is to get the job. If you are being interviewed by native speakers of the language, you will need to learn different conventions. These range from knowing whether you should sit down or wait to be asked, to knowing how to tell when the interview is over. In between there are plenty of other questions. How much are you expected to say in answer to each question? How much should you praise your own virtues? How familiar should you be with the interviewers? How much honesty is valued? The quickest way to find these things out is to ask someone beforehand. This is not a case for learning from experience. By the time experience pays off, your holiday will be over and you'll be back to your studies without a job.

The work culture

Let's say you have landed a job in the tourism industry. Perhaps working in tourism is your ultimate purpose for learning the language. You will want to know areas that can cause misunderstanding because behaviour differs from culture to culture. Here are some common examples which you could try to find out about either through experience or by asking.

In some countries waiters and waitresses, petrol-pump attendants and bus drivers, to name just a few, are seen as people who do a job but are not necessarily there for a conversation. In other cultures it could seem rude not to engage them in some kind of chat.

The question of tipping is part of the same situation. Here are questions tourists might ask you if you are working as a tour guide either in your own country with foreign visitors or elsewhere for people of your own nationality who don't know the language and customs.

If I tip people, does that mean I am seeing them as my inferiors?
If I don't, will the workers miss out on an expected part of their income?
If I do tip, am I expected to say something as I do it?
Is it better to slip it under the bill or give it openly?

Another aspect of the work culture that varies from country to country is the relationship between the worker and the employer. As a student doing a holiday job such as cleaning, you may find yourself quite far down the social scale. If you are doing a menial job you will probably receive the treatment that goes with menial jobs in that particular part of the world.

14.4 Cross-cultural communication

The whole of your language learning is about how to communicate well cross-culturally. It's not so difficult to remember to take your shoes off at the door, if that's what people do, but once the communication starts there are plenty of details to learn.

Tricky situations

At the early stages of second-language learning, students concentrate on how to say all the things they want to say. As they make progress they find themselves in situations where they don't know what to say. The reason may be that there is nothing to say. People find it hard to realise that in some languages there is absolutely no equivalent for something they would say in their own language. For instance, there are languages where people do not accept compliments with words. If someone praises your work or your possessions or your children you simply say nothing. How common are compliments in the language you are studying? Who pays them to whom? What sort of things can be complimented? Are there any taboos?

Think about the language you are studying and try to find out whether people say something, say nothing or use body language in each of these occasions.

You arrive late to a meeting.
Someone has apologised to you.
Just before you start to eat a meal.
When handing someone an object.
Walking in front of someone in a crowded room.

Knowing when and when not to speak is one of the rules of politeness that varies from language to language. Here are some specific ways in which languages have different rules.

Students' reported difficulties

A group of international students living in an English-speaking country offered to say what made it difficult for them to communicate in English even though they had an excellent command of all the vocabulary and structures of the language. Here are some of the points they made. All of these concerns have been well documented in books on cross-cultural communication.

Coming across differently from how you intended

A person wants to show an interest in what is being said and yet doesn't want to appear discourteous or domineering. How are different attitudes conveyed? Often it is something quite specific such as intonation or body language or standing distance. If you are in this situation, one solution is to use the sort of statement that announces your intentions before or after you speak, e.g. 'This probably sounds vague but . . .', and 'Or at least that's the way it seems to me. . . .'

As you watch films in the other language, make a special note of people's body language. Turning down the sound as you watch the first time is one way of noticing how people use their face, gestures and stance to convey different moods. Then the second time, as you listen to the dialogue, check up on your guesses.

Blaming yourself for not understanding

Another feature of cross-cultural communication is that whoever is less fluent in the language will often take the blame for non-understanding, when really it is a shared communication problem and should be clarified in some way. Think of all the ways you ask for clarification in your own language and start using their equivalents in the language you are learning. Some of the ways of sorting out problems are to:

Ask for repetition.
Re-word what the other person has said.
Echo two alternatives ('Did you say . . . or . . . ?').
Carry on with what you think is the topic but be alert for people's responses.

Timing and turn-taking

One politeness rule relates to turn-taking. Language students report that it is often difficult to get a turn to speak because speakers of various languages differ in their rules for timing and turn-taking. Rules can differ from one place to another about:

When to talk and when to listen.
Who should take the initiative in a conversation.
How long to leave before responding (pacing and pausing).
How long to make an answer before giving another person a turn.
Getting a turn to talk.

If you are speaking with native speakers of the language it would be easy to operate by the rules for turn-taking in your own culture. Imagine that there is a discussion going on between three or four friends. How do you know if it is your turn to speak? Do you wait to be asked? Do you take turns? Do you speak whenever you want to? You will probably find this out by observing real conversations, because textbooks make it seem as if conversations proceed smoothly with only minimal interruptions.

If you have a chance to see foreign-language movies, look for answers to these questions.

Do friends interrupt each other while they are speaking?
How do the speakers react to interruptions? Is it a normal part of conversation or seen as rude?
How does one person get a turn if others are talking fast?

Ending a conversation

Another tricky area is getting to the end of the conversation. This is particularly difficult on the telephone where you don't have all the visual clues. Again, films are a good source of ideas.

Choosing and avoiding topics

Knowing whether a topic is appropriate to bring up in a particular situation is another problem. Some people within one culture may be superstitious; others are not. Finding out is not as simple as asking 'Do Spaniards talk about death at the meal table?' Building up your understanding of what topics interest your audience and which actually offend them takes time.

We all know the effect on a gathering of strangers when a child makes a remark that is out of place. In some ways speaking a foreign language is like being a child again. Even when you have the language to say what you want, and an audience to listen, you may feel as if you are picking your way through a minefield. How on earth are you to know whether the speakers of your language want you to ask about their health, their weekends or their incomes?

Unfortunately this information is difficult to come by, especially when textbook dialogues represent one layer of society only. Also, it is much easier to be more aware of the topics that are there in the book than the topics that are missing. One source of information needs to be genuine interactions between native speakers, or at least the interactions that are available to you in novels, short stories and on screen. Another is direct informants. If you are taken to a function such as a wedding by a native speaker, ask questions about any special taboos. Sometimes these relate to superstitions that may or may not bother everyone. If you want to be ultra-careful you will take people's advice even if it does mean erring on the side of caution.

Directness

When someone invites you to agree with their statement, what do you do? In the interests of being cooperative some students report that they have agreed to attend social events that they would really rather not go to, or agreed with statements that they do not believe in. Learning how to be tentative takes time.

Each culture has its own rules about when and how to be direct. Some language students report that they feel it's easy to come across as either too abrupt or too withdrawn. One of the hardest things to understand (and then to start using yourself) in a new language is whether people are using language literally or in other ways. Think of some sentences in English that seem to be doing one thing but actually have another purpose.

1. *Is anyone else around here feeling too hot?*
2. *I was waiting on the corner of Queen St and Victoria St.*
3. *Have you seen the movie . . . yet?*
4. *I've always wanted one of those.*
5. *There's plenty more cake in the tins.*

Before reading on, see how many possible purposes you can think of for each of those comments.

1. *Is anyone else around here feeling too hot?* Is someone suggesting opening a window or going outside or ordering a cool drink? On the other hand they could be complaining indirectly that the air-conditioning installed in the office last week isn't working.

2. *I was waiting on the corner of Queen St and Victoria St.* The person who was standing on the street corner could be complaining ('Why weren't you there?'), or apologising ('Sorry, I was standing in the wrong place.'). Alternatively, it could be that the speaker is launching into an interesting anecdote.

3. The question *'Have you seen the movie . . . yet?'* could be a way of leading in to telling the listener all about the movie, or it could be the start of an invitation to go together to see the movie.

4. The sentence *'I've always wanted one of those'* could be an expression of thanks for a gift received (regardless of whether or not it's the

tenth pair of socks you've received for your birthday), or a request to someone who might buy it, or an expression of longing as two friends are standing staring through a shop window.

5. *'There's plenty more cake in the tins'* could be an offer to keep eating or it could be a sarcastic comment to someone who has just eaten three slices.

As a language learner you need to know how direct or indirect speakers of the language like to be. In some languages it is considered quite rude to come straight to the point, while in others, being indirect gives an impression of deviousness. The same thing applies in refusing social invitations. Should you give the real reason or something that sounds more diplomatic? These are things you can find out either directly, by reading what people have written about comparisons and contrasts between your own language and the one you are learning, or indirectly, as you read genuine conversations, watch movies and listen to native speakers.

Summary of advice

Conveying all those characteristics can be a problem. In our own language and culture we have some control over how others see us. Of course even then there can be misunderstandings, but we have a better awareness that they are happening. We can choose to sort them out if we want to. We know how to signal our mood – how to appear sincere or amused or detached, how to show the negative moods of sarcasm, criticism and insults. We have the whole spectrum of emotions at our fingertips. We can choose to indicate respect or contempt. As well as knowing about politeness and rudeness, we can read the signs that tell who is in control of a topic in a conversational group and when that control moves to another person. We can signal closure to an exchange without being left wondering whether there is still something left to say. We can negotiate our way out of misunderstandings.

Consider this conversation overheard in a park between a male and female student speaking in their own language.

He: Go on. Say it.
She: There's nothing else to say. That's it. I said what I meant.

This sort of exchange usually signals the start of a lengthy unravelling of a problem. How on earth can that be done in a foreign language?

Non-verbal behaviour

Body language is a term used to describe how people use gestures, facial expressions, and how they stand or move in relation to others during conversations. Studies of body language were very popular in the 1970s for people communicating both within and beyond their own cultures. For the foreign-language learner it is more a case of understanding other people's gestures than of trying to turn yourself into a puppet by moving your hands, face and body in unusual ways according to a formula.

Language groups vary in the importance they put on non-verbal behaviour, such as types of dress that signal different occasions, the amount of gesturing they do, the sort of facial expressions that add meaning to words. Some people bow when they meet, some shake hands, others do nothing. Non-verbal behaviour can include the space you leave between yourself and the next person at the party and the amount of touching you are allowed to do with strangers. The list is endless.

Metaphors

Metaphors are one of the hardest aspects of the language to understand and express. It's not just that a particular expression needs to find its equivalent in another language. It's the fact that in speech and in writing, particular language speakers, and in fact groups of people within those speech communities, have preferences for the source of their metaphors. Take sport as an example. In English, many metaphors come from sports: to tackle the question, hit the target, to leap a hurdle. Many are based on the idea of construction: He's building up to something, that comment hit the nail on the head, let's hammer at it until it's solved. Start noticing the source of metaphors in the language you are using. Do they come from nature, from events from the country's past, from religious books or from another source?

Translators have this problem. For example, a translator at an international conference was having a discussion with a speech writer who had sent a copy of his speech ahead of time so that it could be translated into English. Their topic was what to do about metaphors. The translator thought that the language of a speech should sound like the language of the person who wrote it, while the speech writer believed that it should sound like the sort of imagery the listeners were accustomed to hearing in their language. In this case it was even more complicated because many members of the audience had English as their second or third language.

Same occasions, different expressions

So far we have considered general points in cross-cultural communication. Let's look now at how language is used for different purposes in different cultures in three particular situations: gift-giving, ending social visits, and expressing sympathy. As you read the comments, think of the language you are studying, especially the examples you have met of native speakers using the language, such as the dialogue in short stories and novels, or movies.

Offering and accepting gifts

Apart from the choice of what to give to whom on what occasion (or even whether to give a gift at all), the language student has to work out the largely formulaic language of offering and accepting gifts. Which of these statements comes closest to what people would say in the culture you are studying?

I've just brought you this small gift.

This is something very valuable from my country.

A third option would be to say nothing as you hand it over.

The next 'problem' occurs when you have received a gift. What do you say and do as you receive it? Should you open it immediately? How many words of thanks are enough? How do you avoid going too far and sounding insincere? The final part of the conversation (as if the process isn't complicated enough already) is knowing how to respond when the other person has said 'thank you'. The rules may be different for private occasions and public occasions.

Leaving a social visit to someone's home

When you come to the end of a social visit, you need to know first of all whether it is your role or the role of the hosts to signal that the visit is over. Many of us have sat inwardly yawning because we don't want to cause offence by mentioning leaving, while the other party is expecting us to take the initiative.

Then you need to know the language associated with getting out of the door. This ritual usually takes much longer than the brief sentences printed in textbook dialogues. There are phrases for announcing that the visit will soon be over, phrases for summing up the evening, for expressing thanks, for mentioning future meetings and so on. There is even the potentially tricky movement to the door and knowing who leads the way. Remembering to put on your shoes or collect your coat at the end are the least of your worries.

Offering sympathy

The final example is a sadder one and includes spoken and written language. Think of the occasions when people offer sympathy. These are often the same in each culture (death and illness) but the form of expression may vary. The tradition may be that it is best to send a letter, a card with a printed message, flowers or food. At other times a personal visit or a telephone call are more usual. Some of these decisions are better made by consulting someone else on the spot.

CONCLUSION

By way of conclusion, here are the words of someone who spent a year abroad using the language he had studied for many years.

> There are several aspects to *acculturation*. The first is to be aware of what some of the differences are between one culture and another. A second aspect is tolerance or acceptance of ways of doing things that differ from one's own. Then there is the ability to speak and act appropriately in situations where certain behaviours would cause offence. The final step is the longer-term one of coming to appreciate the values and thinking of a new culture.

He doesn't see the kind of adaptation required when one is living in a foreign culture as necessarily involving a loss of identity.

One can step into the sea of another culture and swim in it happily without drowning. The swimmer knows the way out of that culture as well as the way into it.

Note

1. 'English for Newcomers to Australia', Australian Commonwealth Office of Education (revised 1950), quoted by Graeme Kennedy (1983) in his inaugural address 'English for Speakers of other Languages'.

15

LANGUAGE EXAMINATIONS

*Although the ultimate aim of learning a language is to be able to use it outside
the classroom, if you are studying languages as part of a course, then passing the
examination is probably also your goal. In this final chapter we consider the sort
of format you can expect in a language examination and how you could prepare
for it.*

Language examinations (as distinct from literature or linguistics examinations)
usually include both oral and written parts. There is probably not a record of
previous oral examinations, but for the written section the best way to find out
what to expect is to look through old examination papers, after checking that
the format is not going to change for the year you will be sitting. This
information is not secret. Your lecturers or tutors will be able to let you know.
The first half of this chapter explains what to expect from a language examination. In the second half there are more specific techniques, based on actual
language examinations and on advice from successful students.

15.1 THE CONTENT OF THE EXAMINATION

Be sure to read the instructions to the examination. If these are in the
target language you need to have their meaning at your fingertips.
There is a limited number of things they can ask you to do with a
writing exercise (translation, comprehension passage or essay), and you
should be quite familiar with the language of the instructions beforehand. Here are some examples of examination tasks taken from actual
papers and arranged more or less in order of difficulty.

Guided writing

Language exercises are quite varied and are meant to encourage you to make the most of what you know.

Filling the gap

If you are taking a first-year language examination you may be given a piece of text with some gaps in it. This is called a 'close' passage and it may follow a pattern you are familiar with from your classes, in which case you will know what to do. Occasionally an equivalent English word may even be provided. If not, try to see whether the instructions tell you whether you must use just one word or whether a phrase is acceptable.

Even if you are expected to put a single word in each gap, then, if you can't find the actual word, as a last resort it could be worth putting a paraphrase. However, a wrong guess could change the meaning of the whole paragraph. A lot depends on the marking system. Try to find out beforehand whether marks are subtracted for wrong words, in which case you are better to avoid wild guesses. If not, you have nothing to lose except time in putting down a word that just might fit.

It also helps to know whether the exercise calls for just one right answer or whether you could be rewarded for thinking up some unusual idea. Some close exercises are marked on the basis that only one word is right. This is particularly true, of course, if the missing word has a grammatical function. In another type of marking you could lose marks by being particularly clever and original in your choice, while the students who made the more predictable or even boring choices got higher marks.

Dictation

Dictations are another form of guided writing. Although they went out of fashion for a while they are now being used again as a means of checking the connection between students' ability to listen and their command of spelling, and even word breaks. If you have a dictation in an examination it probably means you have also been given them during the year and so you know what to expect. Unlike note-taking, you aim to get everything down, leaving plenty of space for the bits you don't hear the first time around. Writing on alternate lines is a good idea.

In the time between and after the two readings you do your checking, with a close eye for two things – meaning and grammar. If something does not seem to make sense, think again, but don't cross bits out until you have something to substitute. A quick underline reminds you to listen carefully to this bit the second time. Check for the unusual things that can go wrong, such as writing plurals with singulars or changing tenses in odd ways. Practise giving one another dictations before the examination as preparation for the mechanics of writing and keeping up with someone else's pace.

Writing with prompts

In prompted writing you are provided with something to write about, often graphics, such as a series of pictures that tell a story. Again, this is a good test of your ability at the early stages. Perhaps you will be provided with a map marked with an arrow and invited to describe the person's journey. In a German test for beginners, they were told to use a range of prepositions. In another guided piece of writing, students had to re-order words to form a sentence. In that case there was probably only one right answer.

A dialogue is one form of writing which allows you to demonstrate some of the skills of spoken language. Some of these allow you to write whatever you like ('Write a dialogue about the following situation') and others actually provide the words of one speaker all the way through, leaving you to make up the other part. In that case be sure to read the half-dialogue right through first in case there are any surprises at the end.

Free writing

Free writing is different from an essay (see below) in that it is usually shorter and calls for you to use your imagination or draw on concrete events. Topics that you could expect near the beginning of your language studies tend to concentrate on the personal, such as what you did last weekend or where you would like to be in ten years' time. The only restriction in this type of writing has to do with the sentence structure, since one topic tends to steer you into using more of one structure than another.

Translation into and from the language

At the elementary stages the translation may be of isolated sentences, but soon you will move to short passages of text. You can probably find out beforehand whether the passages to be chosen are from books on your reading lists or whether they are completely unseen. If you have not studied translation as a subject, the following general rules could help you.

Before you start translating make a quick assessment of the general topic. Look for clues in the credits at the end. If it is an extract from a newspaper, what is the date and what do you know about that paper's style and readership? If the title and author are missing, then clues may come from the names of the characters and from place names, that indicate time or place. There's nothing more annoying than plunging straight into a translation and then finding in the last sentence a clue that would have made the whole thing much easier.

Leave translating the title until last unless it is quite clearly literal and unambiguous. Translating a title into another language sometimes involves finding completely different words or imagery to convey the meaning. As an example, how would you translate the title 'Toehold on a harbour', which was the title of a piece about a city clinging to the side of a hill?

You will also have to make decisions about terms which have two or more possibilities in the other language. The English terms 'brother' and 'sister' become 'older brother', 'younger sister' etc. in some other languages. If there are no clues in the English version what can you do? Decisions like these shouldn't be left to the moment of the examination. Have some general principles worked out. Usually they will have been discussed in class during the semester or year.

Comprehension

The word 'comprehension' sounds strange to people outside classrooms. It seems to suggest that this is the only part of language learning when you actually have to understand anything. As you will know from years of practice since primary school, a comprehension exercise consists of a section of language, written or spoken, about which you are asked questions. In a language examination the questions will probably be worded in your own language at the earliest stages and then in the target language. The source of the passage could be from literature, from the newspaper or many kinds of spoken language. The more you have read, the better you are prepared for a range of styles. The questions are likely to fall into a pattern. Here are the types to watch for.

Demonstrate understanding of the passage

These questions require you to find information from the passage and are usually (but not always) written in the order the information appears. They may ask what, why, where or how, but you do not have to do any deep thinking to find the answers. Depending on the level of the examination, the questions may be worded differently from the words in the passage. For example, questions that ask about 'the traveller' are tricky if there is no word for traveller in the passage. Keep the whole meaning of the passage in mind.

One helpful thing about recall questions is that they give you a second chance to think about the meaning of the whole passage. In the example above, for instance, it may be that you don't realise anyone is travelling until you read that question and suddenly more of the passage makes sense.

Interpretation

The next level of difficulty is questions that ask you to demonstrate an understanding by finding words in the passage that match a meaning provided, or by saying something in your own words. The question may remind you quite explicitly to use your own words ('What is meant by the term . . . ?') Some of these questions give you a whole sentence to express in another way either in your own or the target language. In this case it is tempting to play around with the words by turning a noun into a verb, but you gain more marks for being original in your paraphrase. Here is an example of avoiding an abstract word you don't know.

Not: There was a shortage of food.
But: People didn't have enough to eat.

At other times you have to find words in the passage:

Find three examples of words that . . .
From the text find synonyms for . . .

Interpretation questions often focus on figurative word meanings and on word plays.

Application

Some questions ask you to take information provided in the passage and apply it to another situation. An example of this type of question could be:

What does . . . tell us about . . . ?
How would you explain . . . to someone who . . . ?

Analysis

Analysing requires you to pick out parts of the information and show
their relevance for something else. In a passage from literature this could
involve finding details that help explain why such and such happened.

What emotions is the reader being asked to feel?
How could this conflict have been avoided?

Combining information to reach a new conclusion

Combining or synthesising information also requires you to look at the
whole passage. For example:

What information do we need to assess the author's claim better?

How do X's actions compare with Y's?

What might have happened if . . . ?

The combining could go beyond the given passage, particularly in a
literature question.

Conclusions can be based on cause and effect ('How many reasons
can you find for . . . ?'), on hypotheses ('Which clues make you
think . . . ?') or on 'What if' suggestions. In answering a question
'Why?', you need to distinguish between the 'why' that calls for a reason
explicitly given in the passage (a recall question) and the 'why' that
invites you to speculate and look for hints. In the latter case you can also
introduce possible causes provided these do not go too far into the
realms of imagination. Save these for your creative essay.

In evaluating viewpoints or actions you are saying something about
their worth. This is the place to draw on all you can remember about the
background: the times, the writer's life and so on. You can, of course,
make comparisons with the present. Although an examination is usually
not the place where people do their most original thinking, it is worth
saying what you really think if that is what you are asked. The key is to
support your answer. You can say 'It seems to me' or 'So and so's
attitude appears to be' but your case will be strengthened if you can

continue with proof from the passage or from reading you have done during the year. It will be even stronger if you are familiar with other works by the same author and can use information from them to support your case. This can be a cunning technique when you are finding it hard to make complete sense of the passage given but you know more about other passages you have studied. The thing to remember here is relevance. You won't be rewarded for writing at length about something you are not asked for.

Essays

The purpose of an essay in the language examination is to test your language ability, rather than your knowledge. However, choosing a topic that you have some knowledge of is obviously an important start. For one thing, you won't waste time wondering what to say. There are two extreme positions students take in writing essays under time limits.

Some decide to restrict themselves only to what they are able to say almost 100% correctly. In this case they use verb tenses they know well and vocabulary where they are sure of the meaning, the spelling and the context. This is the timid approach and may be based on a false premise. Is your essay really being marked negatively, with marks subtracted for each 'error'? This is unlikely at the senior level of a school and even less likely at a university.

What is more probable is that essays are marked for what they show globally of your command of language. The marker will probably be looking for a range of vocabulary, for clever ways of linking ideas and for a range of language structures. In this case the 'simple but accurate' approach will not be rewarded.

Other students go ahead and express ideas that go beyond their language ability, practising the same tactics that work well in conversation. They put words down as best they can, taking a brave stab at the spelling. When they forget a word they leave a blank or even 'create' a word from an English starting point or, more cleverly, based on some other word in the new language. This approach certainly lifts the level of ideas even if it could give an overall impression of carelessness. Discuss your teacher's marking policy beforehand.

A third approach is somewhere in the middle. These students have consciously prepared for the essay questions by revising many useful phrases ('on the other hand', 'a number of factors') and abstract vocabulary ('events', 'features', 'considerations' and so on). This is better than preparing a subject, since subjects are hard to predict. Incidentally, if you have prepared a topic and it isn't given, beware of moulding your prepared piece to fit another topic. Examination markers are quite familiar with irrelevant topics which students under pressure have tried to reshape under a fresh heading. Most can tell the difference between 'The environment under stress' and 'The future of the United Nations' although occasionally students report success with this trick.

Choosing your topic is a stage that needs to be done fairly quickly and without too many regrets halfway through, when you realise another topic would have suited you better. A good range is usually provided and the only ones to avoid totally are those where one word is unfamiliar to you. It could turn out to be the key to the whole meaning. Look out for topics on current issues (local or international), viewpoints about language, cultural concerns, and on personal ambitions and beliefs. Sometimes the topic is suggested in terms of a quotation which invites you to respond with a viewpoint or an expansion of its meaning. Essay topics, unlike the short-paragraph writing discussed earlier, tend to call for opinions rather than for narrative, but again, check with previous papers.

The oral examination

Oral examinations are designed to measure your use of language, rather than your knowledge of a particular subject. You will usually be examined one-to-one with a lecturer, although there are various formats as we'll see. Candidates usually arrive at a fixed time and are given a piece of paper with a topic. The idea is to have a few minutes to collect your thoughts on the topic before being called in. If by any chance the words written on the paper mean absolutely nothing to you, don't panic. An oral examination is not designed to trip you up over one word. Follow the lead of one student who had a piece of paper with the words 'What is your opinion on . . . ?' followed by a word she couldn't remember ever seeing before. Trying to stay calm she made up a sentence to the effect that try as she had, she couldn't think what the word meant. The examiner laughed, told her the meaning in English and then carried on with the interview. All the student had lost was a few minutes of preparation time.

Some examinations now include two students at a time so that they can be assessed on their ability to interact with others while the lecturer does the evaluation. There are one or two traps to watch out for here. If you are rather a shy person you could find yourself out-talked by the other person. An examiner who doesn't hear you talk can't, of course, give you good marks. If, on the other hand, you are the over-talkative one you could find yourself marked down for acting as if you were making a speech rather than observing the rules of conversation.

That leads to a third variation on the oral examination – the class presentation. Students are given topics some time beforehand and told to present them to a group of people, usually their fellow students. This is a good chance to demonstrate what you can do. Nervousness can be a problem. Do as much as you can to overcome it, such as choosing a topic you like, practising in front of a sympathetic friend and making sure that you have enough, but not too much, to say. Ask whether you are allowed to show something as well as talk and whether you are allowed to involve the audience, two ways of deflecting attention from yourself.

15.2 EXAMINATION TECHNIQUES

Doing yourself justice in an examination calls for a combination of study throughout the year, good last-minute preparation, knowing more or less what to expect from an examination, and then following the instructions to the letter. One successful student summed it up like this:

> As for exam preparation . . . I am a great believer in being systematic. I noticed a lot of people study in a very haphazard way and miss a lot of basic things out because of that. I found that finding a native speaker to practise with (and even do some role plays with them) just before an oral test was very effective and made a big difference to my marks. I guess a lot of it was probably to do with confidence and just being 'used' to speaking in Japanese (especially in the first two years that I was learning).

This section expands on his advice about being systematic, doing last-minute practice and calling on all the work you have done earlier in the course.

Study through the year

In one sense this is useless information. Everyone knows in theory that it's better to spread learning out through the year than to do a frantic last-minute attack on it. Although some non-language subjects can be learnt in the last two weeks, in a language examination this is most unlikely.

Last-minute preparation

By 'last minute' we mean the week or two leading up to the examination but as one student said, last-minute preparation does depend on what has gone before.

> I felt that the most effective preparation I did was when I kept detailed notes for the test after each section. That meant at the end of the year I had good notes to revise from and I could study from the parts where I'd done worse. I'd write down the grammar rule with a couple of examples and my notes would say 'Don't write . . . write. . . .' I used plenty of colour coding.

What you can actually revise formally for an examination usually comes down to words and grammatical patterns. One student who was successful in his Japanese examinations had this to say.

> Knowing all the vocabulary – that's the most important. There's nothing more annoying than finding a new word in the text. It really slows you down. It has to be rote learning. You get easy marks through learning all the vocabulary in Kanji – that's guaranteed marks. You need to practise the sentence structures too. There aren't that many until you get to the advanced level.

Then on the day of the examination you need to try and put yourself into the 'mode' of that language.

> Before exams I always try to listen to Spanish music and speak to the cat and myself and my friends only in Spanish. Reading was another important thing.

If you have a different language examination in the morning then you will need to plan ways of switching. Perhaps listening to songs will help.

Dividing up your time

One of the most challenging aspects of taking examinations is managing to finish. In fact, after the point about knowing what to say, it is probably the commonest reason for disappointments. Even straight after students leave the room you hear them saying 'But I knew more. There just wasn't time to write it.'

There are a number of ways of avoiding this trap. The first has already been mentioned. Familiarise yourself with the format of the paper so that you know approximately how many different questions there will be and how many marks each is worth. The number of marks is important. They are usually shown after each question and they allow you to know which sections are worth spending longer on than others.

Another way is to avoid being too immersed in the first couple of questions. Particularly when these are translations, it is tempting to spend longer and longer polishing them up and then failing to attempt a shorter question at the end. If you miss out a question worth 5% then that is 5% down the drain. You simply can't retrieve it. On the other hand, if you have done a passable job on an earlier question, say the translation, then you can be reasonably sure of having 50% and anything else is a bonus.

A third hint has to do with the way you set out your answer on the page. Write double spaced so that additions and corrections can be made easily. Also, if possible you should write on the left hand page only, leaving the right hand page empty. This means that if you do finish early and want to polish up an earlier version then you can start on a fresh page. Make sure that you put a line through the bits you have re-done and only those bits, and wait to draw the line until the rewriting is finished.

Watch out for alternatives

In any examination where there are alternatives, some students are going to get muddled. If it says 'Choose three of the six questions,' someone will hand in six, all of them inevitably half the length or quality required. Even more tricky are those instructions that say 'Answer four questions. You must choose one from Part A and two from Part B.' Think about this type of wording before you go into the exam room and be ready for it.

SUMMARY OF ADVICE

1. Know what to expect.
2. Look carefully at instructions.
3. Keep an eye on the clock.
4. Think of an examination as the chance to show your best.

QUESTIONNAIRE

This book has offered many, many suggestions about strategies for language learning. One way to pull it all together for yourself would be to ask yourself the same sort of questions which students who contributed to this book were asked. One of the students who answered the questionnaire had this to say:

'Actually, after having read through this survey I have re-evaluated myself as a language learner. I am a passive rather than active learner and am surprised that I have done reasonably well given the minimum effort I have put in learning . . .'

Because of her comment, this book concludes with an amended version of the original questionnaire, so that you can measure yourself as a language learner. Many of the amendments come from suggestions from successful students.

Previous language learning

Which languages have you already studied?

What has learning them taught you about the process of language learning?

Motivation for learning a language

How many of these reasons motivate you in your learning of this particular language?

> interest
> being well qualified to start the course

future advantage, e.g., work or travel
the importance of this language world-wide
similarities between this language and others you know
it is easy to learn
it is a heritage language
previous knowledge of the culture, country or language
interest in the culture
opportunities to use the language outside class
liking for the sound of the language

Ability with languages

Here are some of the abilities that students mentioned as helpful for
learning languages. How many of them do you have?

a general talent for languages
a good memory
ability with pronunciation (e.g., enjoying imitating accents)
being a fast reader in your own language
competence in writing in your own language
being good at grammar
an outgoing personality
high motivation
basic curiosity about language

Vocabulary learning

These techniques are expanded in the book. How many of them do you
use to improve your vocabulary learning?

I help myself remember new vocabulary by

- putting words and definitions on cards
- saying the words aloud
- tape-recording the words and listening to them
- making up sentences to use the new words
- memorising textbook sentences using the words
- visualising something that reminded me of the new word

- using memory aids such as rhyming or word-play
- relating the new word to similar words in the new language
- arranging the words on a page in word families

Grammar

Which of these strategies do you use for understanding and using grammar?

- reciting rules
- applying the rules as I made up new sentences
- organising the rules in a new way in my own records
- writing textbook exercises

Listening

How many of these do you listen to?

videos	movies	TV radio songs
tapes provided for you	conversation class	
native speakers	student friends	

Reading

How many of these sources do you read?

textbooks and classwork	bilingual books	easy readers
words of songs	newsletters	magazines
novels	letters from penfriends	journals
advertisements	comics	newspapers

Writing

How many of these strategies do you use?

ask native speakers to mark your writing
swap and discuss each other's assignments

think in the target language, avoiding translation
sound sentences in your head to hear if they sound right
check spelling with a dictionary
apply rules as much as possible then write as you feel it should be
get it corrected and learn from your mistakes
re-use structures met in class

Speaking

Check your speaking strategies against these reported by students:

Read textbook out loud to gain confidence.
Listen to the radio, tape it, speak along with the native speaker.
Make sentences and read them aloud.
Say phrases aloud and in your head in everyday situations.
Use the language laboratory.
Rehearse first what to say, e.g., word order and agreement.
Record yourself.
Self-talk, e.g., about photographs, repeating colloquial sayings out
    loud or in head.
Make up mental conversations while sitting on the bus.
Read something in English and work out how to say it in the other
    language.

FURTHER READING

BOOKS FOR LANGUAGE LEARNERS

The following titles could be interesting to you as a language learner:

Brown, Douglas (1989) *A Practical Guide to Language Learning* (New York: McGraw Hill).

Crystal, David (1987) *The Cambridge Encyclopedia of Language* (Cambridge: Cambridge University Press).

Dufeu, Bernard (1994) *Teaching Myself* (Oxford: Oxford University Press).

Hautrais, Linda, *The Undergraduate's Guide to Studying Languages* (London: Centre for Information of Language Teaching).

Jones, Roger (1991) *Languages and How to Master Them* (Cambridge: Allborough Publishing).

Lewis, Marilyn, and Brown, Pascal (eds) (1993) *Learners Talk: First-hand Accounts of Language Learning* (Auckland: Carrington Polytechnic [now Unitec Institute of Technology]).

Lewis, Marilyn (ed.) (1997) *New Ways in Teaching Adults* (Alexandria, VA: TESOL).

Rubin, Joan, and Thompson, Irene (1994) *How to be a More Successful Language Learner* (Boston, MA: Heinle and Heinle).

REFERENCES

The following books are the basis for the theoretical part of this volume. They have been written for teachers.

Brown, Douglas (1991) *Breaking the Language Barrier* (Yarmouth, ME: Intercultural Press).

Cohen, Andrew (1998) *Strategies in Learning and Using a Second Language* (New York: Longman).

Lightbown, P., and Spada, N. (1993) *How Languages are Learned* (Oxford: Oxford University Press).

Murphey, Tim (1991) *Teaching One to One* (Burnt Mill, Harlow: Longman). This would be a useful book for anyone learning a language with a private tutor.

Nation, I. S. P. (1990) *Teaching and Learning Vocabulary* (New York: Newbury House).

O'Malley, J. M., and Chamot, A. U. (1990) *Learning Strategies in Second Language Acquisition* (Cambridge: Cambridge University Press).

Rost, Michael (1991) *Listening in Action* (Hemel Hempstead: Prentice-Hall).

Wenden, Anita (1991) *Learner Strategies for Learner Autonomy* (Hemel Hempstead: Prentice-Hall).

Wenden, Anita, and Rubin, Joan (eds) (1987) *Learner Strategies in Language Learning* (London: Prentice-Hall).

Williams, Marion, and Burden, Robert (1997) *Psychology for Language Learners* (Cambridge: Cambridge University Press).

Willing, Ken (1989) 'Teaching How to Learn', Macquarie University, Sydney: National Centre for English Language Teaching and Research. (A teacher's book and a book of activity worksheets.)

INDEX